Joseph Krauskopf, Henry Berkowitz

Bible Ethics

A Manual of Instruction in the History and Principles of Judaism

Joseph Krauskopf, Henry Berkowitz

Bible Ethics

A Manual of Instruction in the History and Principles of Judaism

ISBN/EAN: 9783337165185

Printed in Europe, USA, Canada, Australia, Japan

Cover: Foto ©ninafisch / pixelio.de

More available books at **www.hansebooks.com**

BIBLE ETHICS.

A MANUAL OF INSTRUCTION

IN THE

HISTORY AND PRINCIPLES

OF

JUDAISM

According to the Hebrew Scriptures,

BY

Rev. JOS. KRAUSKOPF and Rev. HENRY BERKOWITZ.

CINCINNATI:
BLOCH & CO., PUBLISHERS AND PRINTERS.
1884.

INDEX.

A.—DUTIES TOWARD OUR FELLOW-MEN.

CHAPTER.	PAGE.
I. BE JUST AND KIND,	1
II. CARE FOR THE LIFE, HEALTH AND WELFARE OF OTHERS,	3
III. GUARD THE RIGHTS OF OTHERS,	4
IV. HELP THE NEEDY,	6
V. DO NOT SPEAK OR PLOT EVIL AGAINST ANY ONE,	9
VI. FORGIVE AND FORGET,	14

B.—DUTIES TO OURSELVES.

I. TAKE CARE OF YOUR LIFE AND HEALTH,	16
II. BE INDUSTRIOUS,	17
III. BE TEMPERATE AND CHASTE,	19
IV. BE MASTER OF YOUR TEMPER,	21
V. DESERVE HONOR AND GUARD IT,	23
VI. BE MODEST IN ALL THINGS,	24
VII. KEEP PURE COMPANIONS,	26
VIII. STRIVE TO BE HOLY AND PERFECT,	27
IX. BE CONTENT AND ENVY NO ONE,	28
X. DO CHARITY AND YOU WILL GROW BETTER THEREBY,	30
XI. STUDY YOURSELF THAT YOU MAY BETTER YOURSELF,	31
XII. ELEVATE YOUR MORAL NATURE,	32
XIII. SEEK TO BECOME WISER,	32

C.—DUTIES IN GENERAL.

I. DUTIES OF PARENTS TO CHILDREN,	34
II. DUTIES OF CHILDREN TO THEIR PARENTS,	35
III. DUTIES OF MASTER AND SERVANT,	37
IV. DUTIES TO YOUR BENEFACTORS,	38
V. DUTIES TOWARD ORPHANS, WIDOWS, STRANGERS, OR THOSE OF OTHER BELIEFS,	39

IV. INDEX.

CHAPTER. PAGE.

VI. OUR DUTIES TOWARD OUR COUNTRY, - - - - - - 40
VII. OUR DUTIES TOWARD THE AGED AND HELPLESS, - - - 43
VIII. OUR DUTIES TOWARD THE LOWER ANIMALS, - - - - 44

D.—OUR RELIGIOUS DUTIES.

I. BE EVER MINDFUL OF THE COMMANDMENTS OF GOD AND ACT UP TO
    THEM, - - - - - - - - - - - - - - 46
II. BE FILLED WITH AWE BEFORE GOD THAT YOU MAY DO NO WRONG, 47
III. THOU SHALT LOVE GOD WITH ALL THY HEART, - - - - 50
IV. BE THANKFUL FOR ALL OF GOD'S GOODNESS, - - - 51
V. TRUST FIRMLY IN GOD AND BOW WITH PIOUS HUMILITY TO HIS WILL, 54
VI. BELIEVE IN GOD AND IN NO SUPERSTITION, - - - - 61
VII. WORSHIP GOD WITH AN UPRIGHT HEART, - - - - - 63
VIII. LET THE OBSERVANCE OF THE SABBATHS AND HOLIDAYS, AND YOUR
    ATTENDANCE AT THE PLACE AND PARTAKING IN ALL MATTERS
    OF WORSHIP BE A FIXED AND EARNEST DUTY ALL THROUGH
    LIFE, - - - - - - - - - - - - - - 69

E.—MAN AND HIS MISSION.

I. MAN IS THE NOBLEST OF GOD'S WORKS, - - - - - 74
II. MAN HAS FREE WILL AND CONSCIENCE, - - - - - 76
III. THE SOUL OF MAN IS IMMORTAL, - - - - - - 78
IV. IT IS MAN'S MISSION TO TRY AND PERFECT HIS MORAL, MENTAL AND
    PHYSICAL NATURES, - - - - - - - - - 80
V. IT IS THE DUTY OF EVERY ONE TO SO ACT THAT HIS ACTIONS SHALL
    SERVE AS A MODEL TO OTHERS, - - - - - - 82
VI. IT IS OUR SACRED DUTY TO PRESERVE AND LIVE UP TO OUR INHER-
    ITED FAITH, - - - - - - - - - - 83
VII. IT IS OUR SACRED DUTY TO KEEP FROM SINNING AND TO REPENT
    OF OUR EVIL DOINGS, - - - - - - - - 85
VIII. THE GOOD ARE REWARDED; THE BAD ARE PUNISHED, - - 88
IX. IT IS OUR SACRED DUTY TO OBEY AND TEACH THE WILL OF GOD
    WHICH WAS REVEALED TO ISRAEL, - - - - - 90
X. IN ALWAYS FULFILLING THESE DUTIES LIES THE REALIZATION OF
    THE MISSION OF OUR RELIGION, - - - -

It is the design of this little work to lead up, by progressive steps, to the study of the Bible. Its matter is Biblical. It is the religion and moral code of the Bible which is here taught, freed from the doctrines of theology. This is pure Judaism, but is at the same time that in which Jew and non-Jew agree, because it is religion shorn of that added material in which no two sects entirely coincide.

The method of the book is simple, and will recommend itself as affording the following advantages:

(1) The paragraphs introducing each new theme give, in a terse and simple manner, a clear statement of the principle that is to be learned, thus first stating in familiar terms what is afterward given in the language of the Bible. The beautiful sayings found in the Rabbinical and Talmudical writings are frequently made use of to this end.

(2) Quotations from all sources, in prose and poetry, are given, as containing in a sharp-cut, crystalized form the truths elucidated, presenting them thus in a manner striking, impressive and beautiful. This renders the act of memorizing easy and permanent. At the same time the quotations show how the great men of various ages and nations have expressed themselves concerning these Biblical truths, thus indirectly indicating the vast influence of Jewish thought and the priceless value of the Hebrew tongue, the casket of so many gems.

(3) References to the historical portions of the Bible are made, in order to illustrate by them the principles of practical conduct. The pupil thus has his mind directed to the Bible story for the immediate purpose of searching for the truth, or moral lesson, that has just been

TO THE TEACHER.

set forth to him. The great purpose of teaching Bible history is thus much more effectively gained by first setting the sentiment before the mind and then making the pupil illustrate from the Bible (or any other source, be it profane history, fiction or practical life), than by the method, in common use, of making the story the all-important thing, and pointing dryly at the moral after the interest of the pupil has slackened, his curiosity having been satisfied.

(4) A great abundance of Biblical verses is then given, setting forth the truth that is being learned, in various forms, and presenting it to the mind so as to be seen from all sides. The Bible, the great text-book of the Jewish religion, is thus made to speak for itself. This book is simply an epitome of the Bible. References to the places where the verses are found in the Bible are added, so as to familiarize the pupil with the names of the writers and the books of Biblical literature, and it is expected that he will verify the references by consulting his Bible in each case.

(5) The book is a complete guide in the conduct of life, for old and young, in the family circle, and in all the relations of life, but it is designed especially for Sabbath-school work. The themes handled progress as does also the language with the progress of the pupil. The simpler subjects are first treated of. The daily duties to others are taken up first, so as to direct the child away from itself, and thus nip in the bud its selfish impulses. Then all the other duties in life are explained, proceeding from the more to the less concrete, reserving the more abstract matter for the higher classes and the more matured minds.

(6) There is material enough to supply five classes each with a full year of religious instruction, each division of the book being designed for one year's work, the fifth class to be the "Confirmation Class," by whom the whole book is to be thoroughly reviewed.

(7) Furthermore, this book will be found especially valuable in schools where there is a lack of regularly-trained teachers. This, in fact, is the condition of all our Jewish schools, excepting, perhaps, a few in the larger cities. Any earnest, intelligent person may teach

by this book without having been otherwise specially trained for the task, all the work being clearly prepared for him; but a thorough familiarity with the subjects in the lessons must be obtained by the teacher beforehand, by home study, or, where there is a Rabbi, in normal classes.

(8) Teachers accustomed to the old-style of books for Sabbath-schools will be deceived in not finding the customary collection of prayers, benedictions, hymns, etc. These have been purposely omitted. They will be found in their appropriate places in the prayer-books and hymn-books, and they should be learned from those books. The scope of this book is of a totally different character; it is to teach the religious principles of the Bible. It is not to supplant, in any degree, the books used in divine service.

(9) This book does away with the necessity of using a great many text-books. It is simply accessory to the Bible and the prayer-books, which every one has.

(10) The plan of using the book is:—

(*a*) By direct "talks" between the teachers and the pupils to secure the end of all religious training by shaping and developing the learner's mental, moral and spiritual nature. Ample materials for these "talks" are here offered. Many of the general quotations and of the Bible verses that may be too lofty for the comprehension of children will afford the teacher endless suggestions for those quiet, earnest conversations by which the religious nature can best be reached. Take, as an example, under D: *Our Religious Duties*, the division numbered 6. *Believe in no superstitions*, verse 6, on the various kinds of superstitious practices.

(*b*) *By Illustrations.* Example is stronger than precept. The historical references make no pretense at being complete; they simply point to the way. Every teacher will best know how to spur his pupils on to study the Bible for other illustrations, and to keep careful watch in all reading, and to notice the events of every-day life, with the same end in view, thus awaking their minds, and literally educating, *i. e.*, drawing out their faculties.

TO THE TEACHER.

(*c*) *By Memorizing.* The whole book may well be memorized. The old system, which prevailed in all Jewish schools, of learning a "*Posek*," or a Bible verse each day, was a good one, and should be revived. The book affords ample and suitable material. Where too much matter is given, selections may be readily made. Such a stock of excellent sayings, learned in youth, remains fixed forever, and exercises an influence for good throughout life that can not be estimated.

(*d*) *By Method.* For the smaller schools that are under the disadvantage of having no definite plan of work this book will be found invaluable, inasmuch as it lays out the course of study clearly and methodically.

BIBLE ETHICS.

A.—DUTIES TOWARD OUR FELLOW-MEN.

I.—BE JUST AND KIND.

It is our first duty to be just, which means to be fair to ourselves and to all others. This we can be by giving to every one what is due to him, and by never harming any one, as the wise teacher Hillel said: "What is hateful unto thee, thou shalt not do to others." In being just, we should always be kind. By mercy and gentleness our just acts and words may be made less severe.

> "Kindness is wisdom. There is none in life
> But needs it."—*Bailey.*

"Kindness—a language which the dumb can speak and the deaf can understand."—*Bover.*

> "For blessings always wait on virtuous deeds,
> And though a late a sure reward succeeds."—*Congreve.*

Show the truth of the above from the following or any other stories in the Bible: Genesis xiii. 7–10; Genesis xviii. 17-33; Genesis xxiv.; Genesis xxix. 1–14.

1. Have we not all one Father? hath not one God created us? (then) why shall we deal treacherously, every man against his brother, to profane the covenant of our fathers? (Malachi ii. 10.)

2. Thus hath said the Lord of Hosts, saying: Execute true justice, and show kindness and mercy every man to his brother.

And defraud not the widow or the fatherless, the stranger or the poor; and imagine not evil in your heart, one against the other. (Zachariah vii. 9-10.)

3. He that despiseth his neighbor is a sinner, but he that is gracious to the poor—happiness attend him! (Prov. xiv. 21.)

4. If any person sin, and commit a trespass against the Lord; if he, namely, lie unto his neighbor, in that which was delivered to him to keep, or in a loan, or in a thing taken away by violence, or if he have withheld the wages of his neighbor;

Or if he have found something which was lost, and lie concerning it, and swear falsely in any one of all these which a man can do to sin thereby:

Then shall it be, when he hath sinned and is conscious of his guilt, that he restore what he hath taken violently away, or the wages which he hath withheld, or that which was delivered for him to keep, or the lost thing which he hath found. (Leviticus v. 21-23.)

5. Thus hath said the Lord, Execute ye justice and righteousness, and deliver him that is robbed out of the hand of the oppressor; and the stranger, the fatherless, and the widow shall ye not oppress, and do them no violence, and shed no innocent blood in this place. (Jeremiah xxii. 3.)

6. Thou shalt not avenge nor bear any grudge against the children of thy people; but thou shalt love thy neighbor as thyself: I am the Lord. (Leviticus xix. 18.)

7. Wash yourselves, make yourselves clean: put away the evil of your deeds from before my eyes: cease to do evil;

Learn to do well; seek for justice, relieve the oppressed, do justice to the fatherless, plead for the widow. (Isaiah i. 16-17.)

8. He that walketh in righteousness and speaketh uprightly; he that despiseth the gain of oppressions, that shaketh his hands against taking hold of bribes, that stoppeth his ears against hearing of blood, and shutteth his eyes against looking on evil;

He shall dwell on high; rocky strongholds shall be his refuge: his bread shall be given him; his water shall be sure. (Isaiah xxxiii. 15-16.)

II.—CARE FOR THE LIFE, HEALTH AND WELFARE OF OTHERS.

We must not take the life or injure the health of others, but must do all we can to save and protect them, to better their condition and add to their comfort.

Our own natures are bettered by our trouble in taking care of the welfare of others.

"Take not away the life you can not give,
For all things have an equal right to live."—*Dryden*.

Prove the truth of the above from the following or other stories in the Bible. Examples: Genesis xiv. 1-24; Genesis xviii. 1-8; Genesis xix. 1-4; Exodus ii. 1-21.

---

1. Deliver those that are taken unto death, and those that are moved away to the slaughter hold back. (Proverbs xxiv. 11.)

2. And when you spread forth your hands, I will withdraw my eyes from you, yea, when you make ever so many prayers, I will not hear; your hands are full of blood. (Isaiah i. 15.)

3. No man shall take to pledge, the nether or the upper millstone, for he taketh a man's life to pledge. (Deuteronomy xxiv. 6.)

4. When thou buildest a new house, thou shalt make a battlement for thy roof; that thou bring not blood upon thy house, if any one were to fall from there. (Deuteronomy xxii. 8.)

5. Thou shalt not go up and down as a tale-bearer among thy people; thou shalt not stand (idly) by the blood of thy neighbor; I am the Lord. (Leviticus xix. 16.)

6. Whoso sheddeth man's blood, by man shall his blood be shed; for in the image of God made he man. (Genesis ix. 5-6.)

7. He that killeth a beast shall make restitution for it; and he that killeth a man shall be put to death.

One manner of judicial law shall ye have, the stranger shall be equal with one of your own country; for I am the Lord your God. (Leviticus xxiv. 21-22.)

8. If a man come presumptuously against his neighbor to slay him with guile, from my altar shalt thou take him, that he may die.

And he that smiteth his father or his mother shall surely be put to death.

And he that curseth his father or his mother shall surely be put to death.

And if men strive together, and one smite the other with a stone, or with the fist and he die not but keepeth his bed:

If he rise again and walk abroad upon his crutch, then shall he that smote him be quit; only he shall pay for the loss of his time, and shall cause him to be thoroughly healed. (Exodus xxi. 14–19.)

9. Cursed be he that smiteth his neighbor secretly; and all the people shall say, Amen.

Cursed be he that taketh a bribe to slay a person in innocent blood, and all the people shall say, Amen. (Deuteronomy xxvii. 24–25.)

III.—GUARD THE RIGHTS OF OTHERS.

It is wrong to cheat in buying or selling. It is wrong to deceive any one by speaking or acting lies. All the more is it wrong to rob either in secret or openly, and in any way to do or help to do the least thing against the rights of other people.

> "Oh, what a tangled web we weave,
> When first we practice to deceive."—*Scott.*

"Whatever is right and proper for some, must be so for all."—*I. M. Wise.*

Show that this is true from the following or any other stories in the Bible. Examples: Genesis xix. 4–7 and 9–11; Genesis xxv. 28–34; Genesis iv. 8–9; Genesis xxvii. 1–40; Exodus i. 8–14.

1. Thou shalt not remove the landmark of thy neighbor. (Deuteronomy xix. 14.)

2. Cursed be he that removeth the landmark of his neighbor; and all the people shall say, Amen. (Deuteronomy xxvii. 17.)

3. Remove not the ancient landmark, and into the fields of the fatherless must thou not enter, for their redeemer is strong; he will indeed plead their cause with thee. (Proverbs xxiii. 10–11.)

4. When thou comest into thy neighbor's vineyard thou mayest eat grapes at thine own pleasure, till thou have enough; but into thy vessel shalt thou not put any.

When thou comest into the standing corn of thy neighbor, thou mayest pluck ears with thy hand; but with a sickle shalt thou not move over thy neighbor's standing corn. (Deuteronomy xxviii. 25–26.)

5. If thou sell aught unto thy neighbor, or buy aught of thy neighbor's hand, ye shall not overreach one the other. (Leviticus xxv. 14.)

6. And if a stranger sojourn with thee in your land, ye shall not vex him.

As one born in the land among you, shall be unto you the stranger that sojourneth with you, and thou shalt love him as thyself; for ye were strangers in the land of Egypt; I am the Lord your God. (Leviticus xix. 33–34.)

7. The wicked borroweth, and repayeth not; but the righteous is beneficent and giveth. (Psalm xxxvii. 21.)

8. Balances of deceit are an abomination of the Lord; but a full weight (obtaineth) his favor. (Proverbs xi. 1.)

9. Divers weights are an abomination of the Lord; and a deceitful balance is not good. (Proverbs xx. 23.)

10. Thou shalt not have in thy bag divers weights, a great and a small.

Thou shalt not have in thy house divers measures, a great and a small.

A perfect and just weight shalt thou have; a perfect and just measure shalt thou have; in order that thy days may be prolonged in the land the Lord thy God giveth thee.

For an abomination of the Lord is every one that doth such things, every one that acteth unrighteously. (Deuteronomy xxv. 13–16.)

11. Ye shall not do unrighteousness in judgment, in meteyard, in weight, or in measure. (Leviticus xix. 35.)

12. Whoso divideth with a thief hateth his own soul; he heareth the adjuration and dareth not to tell. (Proverbs xxix. 24.)

13. Ye shall not steal; neither shall ye deny (another's property in your hands), nor lie one to another.

Thou shalt not withhold anything from thy neighbor, nor rob him; there shall not abide with thee the wages of him that is hired, through the night until morning. (Leviticus xix. 11–13.)

14 Woe to those that devise wickedness, and resolve on evil upon their couches! by the first light of the morning they execute it, if they have it in the power of their hand. (Micha ii. 1.)

15. Thus hath said the Lord: Exercise justice on (every) morning, and deliver him that is robbed out of the hand of the oppressor; lest my fury go forth like fire and burn so that none can quench it, because of the evil of your doings. (Jeremiah xxi. 12.)

16. He that declareth the wicked innocent and he that condemneth the righteous, yea both of them are equally an abomination of the Lord. (Proverbs xvii. 15.)

17. Contrive not against thy neighbor any evil, when he dwelleth in safety with thee. (Proverbs iii. 29.)

IV.—HELP THE NEEDY.

We should help along those who are not as well off as we are. Give to every one a chance to live and improve in body and mind A share of all we own really belongs to the poor and needy, and we should freely give to them.

"This mournful truth is everywhere confessed,
Slow rises worth by poverty depressed."—*Samuel Johnson.*

"Every person has a right to live, hence also to the means of support. If one has more than he needs he owes support to him who needs it. To refuse it is indirect robbery. The state, county or municipality must provide for its poor. To render immediate help where it is necessary is the duty of every feeling person."—*I. M. Wise.*

Show that this is true from the following or any other stories in the Bible: Examples: Genesis xviii. 23–32; Genesis xxiv. 17–20; Genesis xli. 9–11; Exodus ii. 16–20; Ruth ii. 9–14.

---

1. Withhold not a benefit from him who is deserving of it, when it is in the power of thy hand to do it.

Say not unto thy neighbor, Go and return, and to-morrow will I give, when thou hast it by thee. (Proverbs iii. 27–28.)

If there be among thee a needy man any one of thy brethren within any of thy gates in thy land which the Lord thy God giveth thee, thou shalt not harden thy heart, nor shut thy land from thy needy brother.

But thou shalt open wide thy hand unto him, and thou shalt surely lend him sufficient for his need, which his want requireth.

Thou shalt surely give him, and thy heart shall not be grieved when thou givest unto him; for because of this thing the Lord thy God will bless thee in all thy work, and in all the acquisition of thy hand.

For the needy will not cease out of the land; therefore do I command thee, saying: Thou shalt open wide thy hand unto thy brother, to thy poor, and to thy needy, in thy land. (Deuteronomy xv. 7, 8, 10, 11.)

3. When thou dost lend thy brother anything as a loan, thou shalt not go into his house to take his pledge.

And if he be a poor man thou shalt not lie down with his pledge.

Thou shalt punctually deliver him the pledge again when the sun goeth down, that he may lie under his own cover, and bless thee; and unto thee shall it be as righteousness before the Lord thy God. (Deuteronomy xxiv. 10–13.)

4. And when ye reap the harvest of your land, thou shalt not wholly reap the corners of thy field, neither shalt thou gather up the gleanings of thy harvest.

And thou shalt not glean thy vineyard, and the single grapes that drop in thy vineyard shalt thou not gather up; for the poor and the stranger shalt thou leave them; I am the Lord your God. (Leviticus xix. 9-10.)

5. When thou cuttest down thy harvest in the field, and forgettest a sheaf in the field, thou shalt not go back to fetch it; for the stranger, for the fatherless, and for the widow shall it be; in order that the Lord thy God may bless thee in all the work of thy hands.

When thou beatest thy olive-tree, thou shalt not go over the boughs again, for the stranger, for the fatherless, and for the widow shall it be.

When thou gatherest the grapes of thy vineyard, thou shalt not glean the small fruit afterward; for the stranger, for the fatherless, and for the widow shall it be. (Deuteronomy xxiv. 19–21.)

6. Is it not to distribute thy bread to the hungry, and that thou bring the afflicted poor into thy house? when thou seest the naked, that thou clothe him? and that thou hide not thyself from thine own flesh?

Then shall break forth as the morning-dawn thy light, and thy healing shall speedily spring forth; and before thee shall go thy righteousness, the glory of the Lord shall be thy reward. (Isaiah lviii. 7–8.)

7. Because I delivered the poor that cried, and the fatherless, yea, that had none to help him.

The blessing of him that was ready to perish came upon me, and the heart of the widow I caused to sing for joy.

I took righteousness as my garment, and it clothed me; as a robe and a mitre was justice unto me.

Eyes was I to the blind, and feet to the lame was I.

A father was I to the needy, and the cause of him I knew not I used to investigate. (Job xxix. 12–16.)

V.—DO NOT SPEAK OR PLOT EVIL AGAINST ANY ONE.

Most of the troubles that people have come from idle talk, with which they fill up their time, instead of doing their duties. Say nothing about your neighbor unless you can say what is good. Try to put yourself in another's place before you judge him. Never flatter.

> "Evil is wrought by want of thought
> As well as want of heart."—*Hood.*
>
> "The evil that men do lives after them."—*Shakespeare.*

Show the truth of the above in the following or other stories in the Bible: Examples: Genesis xxxvii.; Numbers xii. 1–11 and 13–15; Genesis xxvii. 7–40; Numbers xiii., xiv., xxii., xxiii., xxiv.; I. Kings iii.; Esther ii., x.

1. Come, ye children, hearken unto me; the fear of the Lord will I teach you.

Who is the man that desireth life, loveth (many) days, that he may see happiness?

Guard thy tongue from evil, and thy lips from speaking deceit.

Depart from evil, and do good; seek peace, and pursue it. (Psalms xxxiv. 12–15.)

2. A source of life is the mouth of righteousness; but the mouth of the wicked covereth violence. (Proverbs x. 11.)

3. Death and life are in the power of the tongue, and they that love it will eat its fruit. (Proverbs xviii. 21.)

4. The lips of the righteous feed many; but fools die through lack of sense. (Proverbs x. 21.)

5. The heart of the wise maketh his mouth intelligent, and upon his lips he increaseth information.

(Like) the droppings of honey are pleasant sayings, sweet to the soul, healing to the bones. (Proverbs xvi. 23–24.)

6. From the fruit of a man's mouth doth he eat what is good; but the longing of the treacherous is for violence.

He that watcheth his mouth guardeth his soul; but he that openeth wide his lips (prepareth) himself destruction. (Proverbs xiii. 2–3.)

7. Whoso guardeth his mouth and his tongue, guardeth his soul against distresses. (Proverbs xxi. 23.)

8. A man hath joy by the answer of his mouth; and a word (spoken) at the proper time, how good is it! (Proverbs xv. 23.)

9. Like apples of gold among figures of silver is a word spoken in a proper manner. (Proverbs xxv. 11.)

10. Men will kiss the lips of him that giveth a proper answer. (Proverbs xxiv. 26.)

11. Speak not before the ears of a fool; for he will despise the intelligence of thy words. (Proverbs xxiii. 9.)

12. Do not answer a fool according to his folly, lest thou also become equal unto him.

Answer a fool according to his folly, lest he be wise in his own eyes. (Proverbs xxvi. 4–5.)

13. In a multitude of words transgression can not be avoided; but he that refraineth his lips is intelligent. (Proverbs x. 19.)

14. He that holdeth back his speeches hath knowledge; and he that is sparing of his spirit is a man of understanding.

Even a fool, when he keepeth silence, is counted wise; he that shutteth his lips (is esteemed) a man of understanding. (Proverbs xvii. 27–28.)

15. In the transgression of his lips is the snare of the wicked; but the righteous cometh out of distress. (Proverbs xii. 13.)

16. A fool hath no delight in understanding, but in laying open what is in his heart. (Proverbs xviii. 2.)

17. Seest thou a man that is hasty in his words? there is more hope for a fool than for him. (Proverbs xxix. 20.)

18. A fool uttereth all his mind; but the wise holdeth it back. (Proverbs xxix. 11.)

19. I said I will guard my ways that I sin not with my tongue: I will guard my mouth with a muzzle while the wicked is before me. (Psalm xxxix. 2.)

20. For truth uttereth my palate ever, and the abomination of my lips is wickedness. (Proverbs viii. 7.)

21. What is gone out of thy lips shalt thou keep and perform. (Deuteronomy xxiii. 24.)

22. Like silver dross laid over an earthen vessel, so are burning lips with a bad heart. (Proverbs xxvi. 23.)

23. A wicked messenger falleth into unhappiness; but a faithful embassador (bringeth) healing. (Proverbs xiii. 17.)

24. He that hath a froward heart will not find happiness; and he that hath a perverse tongue will fall into evil. (Proverbs xvii. 20.)

25. Remove from the frowardness of mouth; and perverseness of lips put away far from thee. (Proverbs iv. 24.)

26. He that despiseth his neighbor is void of sense; but a man of understanding maintaineth silence. (Proverbs xi. 12.)

27. Carry on thy cause with thy neighbor; but lay not open the secret of another. (Proverbs xxv. 9.)

28. He that walketh about as tale-bearer revealeth secrets; but he that is of a faithful spirit concealeth the matter. (Proverbs xi. 13.)

29. He that goeth about as a tale-bearer revealeth secrets; therefore meddle not with him that enticeth with his lips. (Proverbs xx. 19.)

30. Thou shalt not go up and down as a tale-bearer among thy people. (Leviticus xix. 16.)

31. O Lord, deliver my soul from lips of falsehood, and from a tongue of deceit.

What will (God) give unto thee? or what will he add unto thee, thou tongue of deceit? (Psalms cxx. 2–3.)

32. An abomination of the Lord are lips of falsehood; but they that deal in faithfulness (obtain) His favor. (Proverbs xii. 22.)

33. The lip of truth will stand firm forever; but only for a moment the tongue of falsehood. (Proverbs xii. 19.)

34. The righteous hateth the word of falsehood; but the wicked bringeth shame and dishonor. (Proverbs xiii. 5.)

35. A faithful witness will not lie; but a false witness constantly uttereth lies. (Proverbs xiv. 5.)

36. A deliverer of souls is the true witness; but a witness of deceit uttereth lies. (Proverbs xiv. 25.)

37. A false witness shall not remain unpunished, and he that uttereth lies shall perish. (Proverbs xix. 9.)

38. And if any person sin, because he heareth the voice of adjuration, and he is a witness, since he hath either seen or knoweth something; if he do not tell it, and thus bear his iniquity. (Leviticus v. 1.)

39. If a witness of violence rise up against any man to testify against him for any wrong;

Then shall both the men, who have the controversy, stand before the Lord, before the priests and judges who shall be in those days.

And the judges shall inquire diligently; and behold if the witness be a false witness, he hath testified a falsehood against his brother:

Then shall ye do unto him as he had purposed to do unto his brother; and thou shalt put away the evil from the midst of thee.

And those who remain shall hear and be afraid, and shall henceforth commit no more any such evil thing in the midst of thee. (Deuteronomy xix. 16–20.)

40. And I commanded your judges at that time, saying, Hear the causes between your brethren, and judge righteously between a man and his brother, and between his stranger.

Ye shall not respect persons in judgment; the small as well as the great shall ye hear; ye shall not be afraid of any man; for the judgment belongeth to God. (Deuteronomy i. 16–17.)

41. Thou shalt not receive a false report; put not thy hand with the wicked to be an unrighteous witness.

Thou shalt not follow a multitude to do evil; neither shalt thou speak in cause, to incline after many, to wrest judgment.

Neither shalt thou countenance a poor man in his cause.

Thou shalt not wrest the judgment of thy poor in his cause. (Exodus xxiii. 1–3.)

42. Keep thyself far from a false speech; and him who hath been declared innocent and righteous thou shalt not slay; for I will not justify the wicked.

And thou shalt take no bribe; for the bribe blindeth the clear-sighted, and perverteth the words of the righteous. (Exodus xxiii. 6-8.)

43. These are the things that ye shall do, Speak ye the truth every man to his neighbor; (with) truth and the judgment of peace judge ye in your gates;

And let none of you think evil in your hearts against his neighbor; and love not a false oath; for all these are what I hate, saith the Lord. (Zachariah viii. 16–17.)

44. A godless person is a man of injustice, who walketh with a distorted mouth.

He blinketh with his eyes, he scrapeth with his feet, he pointeth with his fingers.

Perverseness is in his heart, he contriveth evil at all times; he scattereth abroad discord.

Therefore shall suddenly come his calamity; unawares shall he be broken, without a remedy.

Six things there are which the Lord hateth; and seven are an abomination unto his spirit.

Haughty eyes, a tongue of falsehood, and hands that shed innocent blood.

A heart that contriveth plans of injustice, feet that hasten to run after evil.

A false witness that eagerly uttereth lies, and him that scattereth abroad discord among brethren. (Proverbs vi. 12–19.)

45. With his mouth doth the hypocrite destroy his neighbor; but through knowledge are the righteous delivered. (Proverbs xi. 9.)

46. So are the paths of all that forget God; and the hope of the hypocrite will perish. (Job viii. 13.)

47. For the assembly of hypocrites will remain desolate, and fire will consume the tents of bribery. (Job xv. 34.)

48. Even he will come to my assistance; for a hypocrite can not come before him. (Job xiii. 16.)

49. That the triumphal shouting of the wicked is ever of but a recent date, and the joy of the hypocrite endureth only for a moment. (Job xxv. 5.)

50. Hear the voice of my supplication when I cry unto thee, when I lift up my hands toward the most holy place of thy sanctuary.

Snatch me not away with the wicked, and with the workers of injustice, who speak peace with their neighbors with mischief in their heart. (Psalms xxviii. 2-3.)

VI.—FORGIVE AND FORGET.

We degrade ourselves and do wrong to others when we continue to bear ill-will against them.

It is noble to forgive the wrong done us; it is our duty to try and forget the wrong we have forgiven.

> "Good nature and good sense must ever join.
> To err is human; to forgive divine."—*Pope.*

> "The more we know, the better we forgive,
> Whoe'er feels deeply, feels for all who live."—*Madame de Stael.*

> "For it is sweet to stammer one letter
> Of the Eternal's language—On earth it is
> Called, Forgiveness."—*Longfellow.*

Show the truth of the foregoing from the following or any other stories in the Bible: Examples: Genesis xxxiii. 1-17; Genesis xlv.; Numbers xii.; I. Samuel xxiv.; II. Samuel xviii. 24-33; I. Samuel xxiv.; II. Samuel xviii. 33.

1. He that covereth a transgression seeketh love; but he that repeateth a matter separateth confident friends. (Proverbs xvii. 9.)

2. Thou shalt not hate thy brother in thy heart; thou shalt indeed

DUTIES TOWARD OUR FELLOW-MEN.

rebuke thy neighbor and not bear sin on account of him. (Leviticus xix. 17.)

3. Say not, As he hath done to me so will I do to him; I will recompense every man according to his doing. (Proverbs xxiv. 29.)

4. Do not say, I will recompense evil; (but) wait on the Lord, and he will help thee. (Proverbs xx. 22.)

5. If thine enemy be hungry, give him bread to eat; and if he be thirsty, give him water to drink;

For though thou gatherest coals of fire upon his head, yet will the Lord repay it unto thee. (Proverbs xxv. 21–22.)

6. If thou meet thine enemy's ox or his ass going astray, thou shalt surely bring it back to him again.

If thou see the ass of him that hateth thee lying under his burden, and wouldst forbear to unload him, (thou must not do so, but) thou shalt surely unload with him. (Exodus xxiii. 4–5.)

7. At the fall of thine enemy do not rejoice; and at his stumbling let not thy heart be glad. (Proverbs xxiv. 17.)

8. This also were an iniquity punishable by a judge; for thus would I have denied the God that is above.

If I ever rejoice at the downfall of him that hated me, or was elated when evil befell him;—

But I suffered not my mouth to sin by denouncing with a curse his soul. (Job xxxi. 28–30.)

9. When the Lord receives a man's ways in favor, he causeth even his enemies to be at peace with him. (Proverbs xvi. 7.)

B.—DUTIES TO OURSELVES.

I.—TAKE CARE OF YOUR LIFE AND HEALTH.

The most wonderful thing in the world is our own life. No one can explain it. Each one of us is placed here in the world, some are strong, some are weak; but whatever are our powers, they are the gift of God, and may give us great joy if they are rightly used.

It is our sacred duty to care for this life which God has lent us. We must be very careful of our bodies, must not go into danger foolishly, but must exercise freely in the open air and do everything we can to keep in good health and to gain strength.

Without good health and strength we can never do those duties which every one ought to do; we can not improve our minds as we should, nor can we be of as much good to others as we ought to be. Therefore, we must hold it to be our first duty to ourselves to take care of life and health.

"Know, all the good that individuals find,
Or God and nature meant to mere mankind,
Reason's whole pleasure, all the joys of sense,
Lie in three things—Health, Peace and Competence."—*Pope.*

"A sacred burden is the life ye bear,
Look on it, lift it, bear it solemnly,
Stand up and walk beneath it steadfastly;
Fail not for sorrow, falter not for sin,
But onward, upward, till the goal ye win."
—*Frances Anne Kemble.*

Give examples from your own observations and readings:
1. Take exceeding good care of yourselves. (Deuteronomy iv. 15.)

2. The merciful man doeth good to his own soul, but he that is cruel, troubleth his own flesh. (Proverbs xi. 17.)

3. Worriment in the heart of man maketh it droop, but a good word will make it glad. (Proverbs xii. 25.)

II.—BE INDUSTRIOUS.

Our wise men said: "Love work. Work is great, for it supports man. Work is great, for it honors man. To have learning and not put it to use is wrong. He who fails to have his child learn some useful trade, brings him up to lead a sinful life. It is beautiful to have learning and yet be skillful at a trade; the use of both together will keep one from sin. Every father must have his son learn the law of God and also a trade. Man is born to work."

All these sayings are true. Though idleness seems pleasant, yet it surely leads to sin and misery. Only through working can we be truly happy. By working we earn our own living and, so, are kept from begging, or from living upon the means of others. By working we get strong and keep our health, and can do our share in looking after the welfare of the sick and the helpless. But the idler neglects himself, is useless to others and is easily led to sin. To be idle is a shame; to work is an honor. Indeed, work makes us more and more perfect, for, as our teachers have again said: "Industry brings purity; purity, cleanness; cleanness, holiness; holiness, humbleness; humbleness, fear of sin; fear of sin, Godliness."

"Absence of occupation is not rest,
A mind quite vacant is a mind distressed."—*Cowper*.

Example: Genesis xxxii. 10–12.

---

1. Sweet is the sleep of the laboring man, whether he eat little or

much; but the abundance of the rich will not permit him to sleep. (Ecclesiastes v. 11.)

2. And the Lord God took the man and put him in the garden of Eden to work it and to guard it. (Genesis ii. 15.)

3. In the sweat of thy face shalt thou eat bread. (Genesis iii. 19.)

4. He that tilleth his land shall be satisfied with bread; but he that followeth vain persons is void of understanding. (Proverbs xii 11.)

5. Love not sleep lest thou come to poverty; open thine eyes and thou shalt be satisfied with bread. (Proverbs xx. 13.)

6. He becometh poor that dealeth with a slack hand; but the hand of the diligent maketh rich. He that gathereth in summer is a wise son; but he that sleepeth in harvest is a son that causeth shame. (Proverbs x. 4-5.)

7. The hand of the diligent shall rule; but the slothful shall be under tribute. (Proverbs xii. 24.)

8. For thou shalt eat the labor of thy hands; happy shalt thou be and it shall be well with thee. (Psalms cxxviii. 2.)

9. In order that the Lord thy God may bless thee in all the work of thy hand which thou doeth. (Deuteronomy xiv. 29.)

10. Seest thou a man diligent in his work, before kings he shall stand. (Proverbs xxii. 29.)

11. Prepare thy work without, and make it fit for thyself in the field, and afterward build thy house. (Proverbs xxiv. 27.)

12. He that tilleth his land shall have plenty of bread; but he that followeth after vain persons shall have poverty enough. (Proverbs xxviii. 19.)

13. On account of the cold the sluggard will not plow; therefore, shall he beg in the harvest and shall have nothing. (Proverbs xx. 4.)

14. By the field of a slothful man I passed and by the vineyard of a man void of understanding. And lo! it was all grown over with thorns, and nettles had covered the face thereof, and the stone fence thereof was broken down. Then I saw and considered it well, I looked upon it and received instruction. (Proverbs xxiv. 30-32.)

15. Go to the ant, thou sluggard, consider her ways and be wise.

Which, having no guide, overseer or ruler, provideth in the summer her bread, and gathereth in the harvest her food. How long, oh sluggard, wilt thou sleep, when wilt thou arise from thy slumbers? Yet a little sleep, a little slumber, a little folding of the hands in sleep. So shall thy poverty come like a traveler, and thy want as an armed man. (Proverbs vi. 6-11.)

16. Slothfulness casts into a deep pit, and an idle soul shall suffer hunger. (Proverbs xix. 15.)

17. The longing of the slothful one killeth him, for his hands refuse to work. (Proverbs xxi. 25.)

18. By much slothfulness the beams will decay, and through idleness of the hands, the house will drop through. (Ecclesiastes x. 18.)

19. He also that is slothful in his work is brother to him that is a great waster. (Proverbs xviii. 9.)

20. The way of the slothful man is as a hedge of thorns; but the way of the righteous is made level. (Proverbs xv. 19.)

21. The slothful man says: "There is a lion without; I shall be slain in the streets." (Proverbs xxii. 13.)

22. The slothful man says: "There is a lion in the way, a lion is in the streets. As the door turneth on its hinges so doth the slothful upon his bed. The slothful hideth his hand in his bosom; it wearieth him to bring it again to his mouth. The sluggard is wiser in his own conceit than seven men that can give a reason. (Proverbs xxvi. 13-16.)

III.—BE TEMPERATE AND CHASTE.

Enjoy the gifts of nature, God has given them to us that we may enjoy them. But they will not be enjoyable unless we are moderate and reasonable in their use. Too much of anything is not good. Be chaste, that is, be pure of heart in all your desires and then you will be temperate in all your enjoyments.

> "Where lives the man that has not tried
> How mirth can into folly glide,
> And folly into sin?"—*Scott.*

"Well observe
The rule of not too much, by temperance taught
In what thou eat'st and drink'st."—*Milton.*

Examples: I. Samuel ii. 12-17.

1. Keep thy heart with all diligence; for out of it are the issues of life. (Proverbs iv. 23.)
2. All the days of the afflicted are evil; but he that is of good heart hath a feast continually. (Proverbs xv. 15.)
3. And thou shalt rejoice in every good thing which the Lord thy God hath given unto thee and unto thy house, thou and the Levite and the stranger that is among you. (Deuteronomy xxvi. 11.)
4. And thou shalt rejoice before the Lord thy God in all that thou puttest thy hand unto. (Deuteronomy xii. 18.)
5. And the land shall yield her fruit and ye may eat your fill. (Leviticus xxv. 19.)
6. It is not good to eat much honey. (Proverbs xxv. 27.)
7. According to their pasture so they were filled; they were filled and their heart was exalted; therefore, have they forgotten me. (Hosea xiii. 6.)
8. Woe unto them that rise early in the morning in order that they may follow strong drink; that continue until night till wine inflame them! And the harp and the viol, and the tabret and pipe and wine are in their feasts, but they regard not the work of God and the doings of his hands they do not see. (Isaiah v. 11-12.)
9. Woe unto them that are mighty to drink wine and men of valor to mix strong drink. (Isaiah v. 22.)
10. Wine is a mocker, strong drink is raging; whosoever is deceived thereby is not wise. (Proverbs xx. 1.)
11. A man of want shall he become that loveth pleasure; he that loveth wine and oil shall not be rich. (Proverbs xxi. 17.)
12. Be not among wine-bibbers; among riotous eaters of flesh. For the drunkard and glutton shall come to poverty, and drowsiness shall clothe a man with rags. (Proverbs xxiii. 20-21.)

13. Who hath woe? Who hath sorrow? Who hath quarreling? Who hath idle talk? Who hath wounds without cause? Who hath redness of eyes? They that tarry long at the wine; those that go to seek mixed wine. Look not thou upon the wine when it is red, when it giveth to the cup its color, when it goeth down smoothly. At last it biteth like a serpent and stingeth like an adder. (Proverbs xxiii. 29-32.)

14. Whoso keepeth the law is a wise son; but he that is a companion of riotous men shameth his father. (Proverbs xxviii. 7.)

IV.—BE MASTER OF YOUR TEMPER.

In speaking and in answering we should always be calm, patient, peaceful and gentle to our companions and relatives, as, indeed, to every one, high or low, rich or poor. "He who can always do this," said one of our wise teachers, "will be beloved in heaven as well as on earth."

"Of all bad things by which mankind are cursed,
Their own bad tempers surely are the worst."—*Cumberland.*

"Control your passion or it will control you."—*Horace.*

---

1. The discretion of a man deferreth his anger, and it is his glory to pass over a transgression. (Proverbs xix. 11.)
2. He that is slow to wrath is of great understanding; but he that is hasty of spirit exalteth folly. (Proverbs xiv. 29.)
3. A soft answer turneth away wrath; but grievous words stir up anger. (Proverbs xv. 1.)
4. By long forbearing is a prince persuaded, and a soft tongue breaketh the bone. (Proverbs xxv. 15.)
5. Strive not with a man without cause if he have done thee no harm. (Proverbs iii. 30.)
6. And Abram said unto Lot: "Let there be no strife, I pray

thee, between me and thee, and between my herdsmen and thy herdsmen; for we be brethren." (Genesis xiii. 8.)

7. Go not forth hastily to strive, lest thou know not what to do in the end thereof, when thy neighbor hath put thee to shame. (Proverbs xxv. 8.)

8. He that passeth by and meddleth with strife belonging not to him, is like one that taketh a dog by the ears. (Proverbs xxvi. 17.)

9. He loveth transgression that loveth strife, and he that exalteth his gait seeketh destruction. (Proverbs xvii. 19.)

10. A wrathful man stirreth up strife, ; but he that is slow to anger appeaseth strife. (Proverbs xv. 18.)

11. Deceit is in the heart of them that imagine evil; but to the counselors of peace is joy. (Proverbs xii. 20.)

12. Better is a dry morsel and quietness therewith than a house full of sacrifices with strife. (Proverbs xvii. 1.)

13. It is an honor for a man to cease from strife; but every fool will be meddling. (Proverbs xx. 3.)

14. A fool's wrath is presently known; but a prudent man covereth shame (Proverbs xii. 16.)

15. A stone is heavy, and the sand weighty; but a fool's wrath is heavier than them both. (Proverbs xxvii. 3.)

16. Be not hasty in thy spirit to be angry; for anger resteth in the bosom of fools. (Ecclesiastes vii. 9.)

17. Cease from anger and forsake wrath; fret not thyself in anywise to do evil. For evildoers shall be cut off; but those that wait upon the Lord, they shall inherit the earth. (Psalms xxxvii. 8–9.)

18. An angry man stirreth up strife, and a furious man aboundeth in transgression. (Proverbs xxix. 22.)

19. As coals are to burning coals, and wood to fire, so is a contentious man to kindle strife. (Proverbs xxvi. 21.)

20. Make no friendship with an angry man; and with a furious man thou shalt not go; lest thou learn his ways, and get a snare to thy soul. (Proverbs xxii. 24–25.)

V.—DESERVE HONOR AND GUARD IT.

Strive always to be manly and womanly. To be so you must, above all, try to learn for yourself, think for yourself, speak and act for yourself. Do not follow any one blindly. Above all, do nothing and say nothing which is to gain you favor by injuring another. Be no hypocrite. Live up to what you believe and give it up at no cost. Suffer everything rather than the loss of your honor. If you thus strictly keep up your own respect and honor, others will feel bound to pay you honor.

"There are three crowns," said our teachers, "the crown of the king, for power, the crown of the scholar, for learning, the crown of the priest, for holiness; but there's another, the crown of a good name, which excels them all."

> " Honor is purchased by deeds we do,
> * * * *   honor is not won,
> Until some honorable deed is done."—*Marlowe.*

> " When honor comes to you, be ready to take it;
> But reach not to seize it before it is near."—*John Boyle O'Reilly.*

> " Honor and shame from no condition rise;
> Act well your part, there all the honor lies."—*Pope.*

1. Better is the poor that walketh in his integrity than he that is perverse in his lips, and is a fool. (Proverbs xix. 1.)
2. A good name is better than precious ointment; and the day of death than the day of one's birth. (Ecclesiastes vii. 1.)
3. A good name is rather to be chosen than great riches, and loving favor rather than silver and gold. (Proverbs xxii. 1.)
4. The memory of the just is blessed; but the name of the wicked shall rot. (Proverbs x. 7.)

5. As snow in summer, as rain in harvest, so honor is not seemly for a fool. (Proverbs xxvi. 1.)

VI.—BE MODEST IN ALL THINGS.

When we think of how great the world is, and how small we are, when we look out over the land with its endless forms of trees and plants and animals; still more, if we are out upon the vast ocean with nothing but water to be seen, only over head the thousands of glistening stars that we never can reach, then we feel deeply how great God is and how weak man is. If we keep this feeling always awake within us, and these truths always before our minds, it will make us humble and modest in all our aims, words and conduct, for it makes us feel that pride, overbearing manners and conceit are vain, foolish, silly and even disgusting.

> " In the sweat of thy face shalt thou eat bread,
> Till thou return unto ground; for thou
> Out of the ground wast taken; know thy birth,
> For dust thou art, and shalt to dust return."—*Milton.*

Examples: Numbers xi. 25-30. I. Samuel xvii.

1. Let another man praise thee, and not thine own mouth; a stranger, and not thine own lips. (Proverbs xxvii. 2.)
2. The fear of the Lord is the instruction of wisdom; and before honor is humility. (Proverbs xv. 33.)
3. He hath shown thee, O man, what is good; and what doth the Lord require of thee, but to do justly, and to love mercy and to walk humbly with thy God? (Micha vi. 8.)
4. But the meek shall inherit the earth; and shall delight themselves in the abundance of peace. (Psalms xxxvii. 11.)

DUTIES TO OURSELVES.

5. The meek also shall increase their joy in the Lord, and the poor among men shall rejoice in the holy one of Israel. (Isaiah xxix. 19.)

6. Seek ye the Lord, all ye meek of the earth, which have wrought his judgment; seek righteousness, seek meekness; it may be ye shall be hid in the days of the Lord's anger. (Zephaniah ii. 3.)

7. When pride cometh, then cometh shame; but with the lowly is wisdom. (Proverbs xi. 2)

8. Put not forth thyself in the presence of the king, and stand not in the place of great men; for better it is that it be said unto thee, "Come up hither," than that thou shouldst be put lower in the presence of the prince whom thine eyes have seen. (Proverbs xxv. 6-7.)

9. A man's pride shall bring him low; but honor shall uphold the humble in spirit. (Proverbs xxix. 23.)

10. Pride goeth before destruction, and a haughty spirit before a fall. Better it is to be of an humble spirit with the lowly, than to divide the spoil with the proud. (Proverbs xvi. 18-19.)

11. Every one that is proud in heart is an abomination to the Lord; though hand join in hand, he shall not be unpunished. (Proverbs xvi, 25.)

12. The Lord will destroy the house of the proud; but he will establish the border of the widow. (Proverbs xv. 25.)

13. Now the man Moses was very meek, above all the men which were upon the face of the earth. (Numbers xii. 3.)

14. And Moses said unto God: "Who am I, that I should go unto Pharoah, and that I should bring forth the children of Israel out of Egypt?" (Exodus iii. 11.)

15. And Moses said unto the Lord: "O my Lord, I am not eloquent, neither heretofore, nor since thou hast spoken unto thy servant; but I am slow of speech, and of a slow tongue." And he said, "O my Lord, send, I pray thee, by the hand of him whom thou wilt send." (Exodus iv. 10, 13.)

16. And Moses said unto him: "Art thou so zealous for me? would to God that all the Lord's people were prophets, and that the Lord would put his spirit upon them." (Numbers xi. 29.)

VII.—KEEP PURE COMPANIONS.

We are judged by the company we keep. Associate, therefore, only with those who are good and those who are sensible and wise, so that you may become like them. Have the courage to say "No," when you are tempted into evil ways. Tremble before the first misstep, for after it is made there are but a few strides before your fall. Many think that they may go into the company of evildoers but withdraw when they please. This is not so. Once we begin we are counted with them and can rarely get away; soon the best of us become bad, however well we are brought up at home and in school.

Be not thoughtless; think of the great grief he brings upon his parents, relatives, teachers and friends, and how miserable he makes himself, who goes into bad company and at last comes to shame, who is disgraced in public before all people and in private before his own conscience.

> " Vice is a monster of so frightful mien,
> As to be hated, needs but to be seen;
> Yet seen too oft, familiar with her face
> We first endure, then pity, then embrace."—*Pope*

Examples: I. Kings xii.; II. Chronicles xxii.; Numbers xi. 24-29.

1. A man that hath friends must show himself friendly; and there is a friend that sticketh closer than a brother. (Proverbs xviii. 24.)
2. He that loveth pureness of heart, for the grace of his lips, the king shall be his friend. (Proverbs xxii. 11.)
3. I have not sat with vain persons, neither will I go in with dissemblers. I have hated the congregation of evildoers, and will not sit with the wicked. (Psalms xxvi. 4-5.)
4. It is better to hear the rebuke of the wise than for a man to hear the song of fools. (Ecclesiastes vii. 5.)

5. A violent man enticeth his neighbor and leadeth him into the way that is not good. (Proverbs xvi. 29.)

6. Enter not into the path of the wicked, and go not in the way of evil men. Avoid it, pass not by it, turn from it, and pass away. For they sleep not, except they have done mischief; and their sleep is taken away, unless they cause some to fall. For they eat the bread of wickedness, and drink the wine of violence. (Proverbs iv. 14-17.)

7. Discretion shall preserve thee, understanding shall keep thee; to deliver thee from the way of the evil man, from the man that speaketh froward things; from those who leave the paths of uprightness to walk in the ways of darkness; who rejoice to do evil, and delight in the frowardness of the wicked; whose ways are crooked, and they froward in their paths. (Proverbs ii. 11-15.)

8. My son, if sinners entice thee, consent thou not. If they say, "Come with us, let us lay wait for blood, let us lurk privily for the innocent without cause, let us swallow them up alive as the grave, and whole as those that go down into the pit; we shall find all precious substance, we shall fill our houses with spoil; cast in thy lot among us; let us all have one purse"; my son, walk not thou in the way with them; refrain thy foot from their path. (Proverbs i. 10-15.)

9. Be not thou envious against evil men, neither desire to be with them, for their heart studieth destruction, and their lips talk of mischief. (Proverbs xxiv. 1-2.)

10. Blessed is the man that walketh not in the counsel of the ungodly, nor standeth in the way of sinners, nor sitteth in the seat of the scornful. (Psalms i. 1.)

VIII.—STRIVE TO BE HOLY AND PERFECT.

To be free from sin and to do what is right and good, is to be holy. It is our selfishness that makes us want to do wrong. We must seek to overcome it, and thus by keeping from sin, by doing good to every one, whatever be his religion, his opinions or his race, and becoming wiser each day, we may grow more and more perfect or godlike.

> "He that has light within his own clear breast
> May sit in the center and enjoy bright day;
> But he that hides a dark soul and foul thoughts,
> Benighted walks under the midday sun."

1. Sanctify yourself and be ye holy, for I am the Lord your God, and ye shall keep my statutes and do them. I am the Lord who sanctifies you. (Leviticus xx. 7–8.)

2. He that followeth after righteousness and mercy, findeth life, righteousness and honor. (Proverbs xxi. 21.)

3. Moreover, thou shalt provide out of all the people able men, such as fear God, men of truth, hating covetousness, and place such over them. (Exodus xviii. 21.)

4. Incline my heart unto thy testimonies, and not to covetousness. (Psalms cxix 36.)

5. For what is the hope of the hypocrite, though he hath gained, when God taketh away his soul? Will God hear his cry when trouble cometh upon him? Will he delight himself in the Almighty? Will he always call upon God? (Job xxvii. 8–10.)

IX.—BE CONTENT AND ENVY NO ONE.

Most people are always busy trying to earn money, and yet are never satisfied when they have it. It is right to earn money honestly, for with it we can do good to ourselves and to others; but "only he is rich," said our Rabbis, "who makes good use of his riches."

The most miserable person is he who is envious of another's wealth, success or pleasures. He can not enjoy what he has, because of his fretting for what he has not. Let us never be envious, but remember that contentment is the only true wealth.

> "My crown is in my heart, not on my head,
> Not decked with diamonds and Indian stones,
> Not to be seen; my crown is called *Content*,
> A crown it is that seldom kings enjoy."—*Shakespeare*.

> " Happy the man, of mortals happiest he
> Whose quiet mind from vain desires is free;
> Whom neither hopes deceive nor fears torment,
> But lives at peace, within himself content;
> In thought or act accountable to none
> But to himself and to his God alone."—*George Granville.*

Show that this is true from the following or other stories of the Bible:
I. Samuel xviii.

---

1. Better is little with the fear of the Lord than great treasure and trouble therewith. (Proverbs xv. 16.)
2. Better is a little with righteousness than great revenues without right. (Proverbs xvi. 8.)
3. Better is the poor that walketh in his uprightness than he that is perverse in his ways, though he be rich. (Proverbs xxviii. 6.)
4. The rich and the poor meet together, the Lord is the maker of them all. (Proverbs xxii. 2.)
5. Be thou not afraid when one is made rich, when the glory of his house is increased; for when he dieth he shall carry nothing away, his glory shall not descend after him. (Psalms xlix. 17-18.)
6. He that trusteth in his riches shall fall, but the righteous shall flourish as a branch. (Proverbs xi. 28.)
7. A little that the righteous man has is better than the riches of many wicked. For the arms of the wicked shall be broken, but the Lord upholdeth the righteous. The Lord knoweth the days of the upright, and their inheritance shall be forever. They shall not be ashamed in the evil time, and in the days of famine they shall be satisfied. (Psalms xxxvii. 16-19.)
8. I have been young, and now I am old; yet have I not seen the righteous forsaken, nor his seed begging bread. (Psalms xxxvii. 25)
9. He that hasteth to be rich, hath an evil eye, and considereth not that poverty shall come upon him. (Proverbs xxviii. 22.)
10. A faithful man shall abound with blessings, but he that maketh haste to be rich shall not be innocent. (Proverbs xxviii. 20.)

11. Two things have I required of thee, deny me them not before I die. Remove far from me vanity and lies, give me neither poverty nor riches, feed me with food convenient for me, lest I be full and deny thee, and say, "Who is the Lord?" or lest I be poor and steal, and take the name of my God in vain. (Proverbs xxx. 7-9.)

12. Better is a dinner of herbs, where love is, than a stalled ox and hatred therewith. (Proverbs xv. 17.)

13. Let not thine heart envy sinners; but be thou in the fear of the Lord all day long. (Proverbs xxiii. 17.)

X.—DO CHARITY AND YOU WILL GROW BETTER THEREBY.

There is a blessing in doing good to others which makes us feel richer than any amount of wealth can When we treat our visitors and friends hospitably it ennobles us, as does also giving to the poor.

To do charity is our duty indeed, but even a gift can be made irreligious by its being done in an unwilling spirit, in an unfriendly or in a showy manner. To make a show of one's charity, our sages taught, is sinful, for it not only debases us, but it shames the helpless ones. "Charity is a virtue of the heart and not of the hands." Such charity we can all show by constant kindness in words and acts.

> "In 'faith' and 'hope' the world will disagree,
> But all mankind's concern is Charity.
> All must be false that thwart this one great end,
> And all of God, that bless mankind or mend."

1. He that hath pity upon the poor lendeth to the Lord, and that which he hath given will he pay him again. (Proverbs xix. 17.)

2. He that hath a bountiful eye shall be blessed; for he giveth of his bread to the poor. (Proverbs xxii 9.)

3. He that giveth unto the poor shall not lack, but he that hideth his eyes shall have many a curse. (Proverbs xxviii. 27.)

4. Treasures of wickedness profit nothing, but righteousness (charity) delivereth from death. (Proverbs x. 2.)

5. He that is greedy troubleth his own house, but he that hateth gifts shall live. (Proverbs xv. 27.)

6. The vile person shall be no more called liberal, nor the churl said to be bountiful. For the vile person will speak villainy, and his heart will work iniquity, to practice hypocrisy, and to utter error against the Lord, to make empty the soul of the hungry, and he will cause the drink of the thirsty to fail. The instruments also of the churl are evil, he deviseth wicked devices to destroy the poor with lying words, even when the needy speaketh right. But the liberal deviseth liberal things, and by liberal things shall he stand. (Isaiah xxxii. 5–8.)

XI.—STUDY YOURSELF THAT YOU MAY BETTER YOURSELF.

We usually talk about the faults of others but fail to think of our own. This is unwise and leads to trouble. We should study ourselves and try to remove the faults we have.

"Know thyself and be wise are the same thing."

"Go to your heart,
Knock there; and ask your heart what it
Doth know."—*Shakespeare*.

"Ere you remark another's sin
Bid thine own conscience look within."—*Gay*.

"It is in general more profitable to reckon up our defects than to boast of our attainments."—*Carlyle*.

1. Create in me a clean heart, O God; and renew a right spirit within me. (Psalms li. 10.)

2. Let us search and try our ways, and turn again to the Lord. Let us lift up our heart with our hands unto God in the heavens. (Lamentations iii. 40-41.)

3. Keep thy heart with all diligence; for out of it are the issues of life. (Proverbs iv. 23.)

XII.—ELEVATE YOUR MORAL NATURE.

In the worry and toil of our every-day lives we must not let our spirits sink. The selfishness and ill will of others may give us trouble, we may find ourselves slipping back into bad habits and ways, but we must never lose courage. Let us be strong in our will to do good and continue in trying to lift ourselves above all error and sin.

> "What the superior man seeks is in himself;
> What the small man seeks is in others."—*Confucius.*

> "Character is higher than intellect."—*Emerson.*

> "Stand fast and all temptation to transgress repel."—*Milton.*

"The true grandeur of humanity is in moral elevation, sustained, enlightened and decorated by the intellect of man."—*Charles Sumner.*

1. Examine me, O Lord, and prove me; try my thoughts and my heart, for thy loving kindness is before mine eyes; and I have walked in thy truth. (Psalms xxvi. 2–3.)
2. A merry heart maketh a cheerful countenance; but by sorrow of the heart the spirit is broken. (Proverbs xv. 13.)
3. A merry heart doeth good like a medicine; but a broken spirit drieth the bones. (Proverbs xvii. 22.)

XIII.—SEEK TO BECOME WISER.

"Having wisdom what do I lack? Lacking wisdom what have I?" asked the Rabbis. To become wise should be our constant aim, but the first thing is to keep in mind how very ignorant even the wisest among us is. It is not so much the knowing many things that makes us wise, for even from the humblest person we may learn something new; no, it is rather being firm in our minds and strong in ruling ourselves. Wisdom shows itself in our deeds as much as in our speaking.

DUTIES TO OURSELVES.

"Wisdom adorns riches and overshadows poverty."—*Socrates.*

"By wisdom wealth is won;
But riches purchased wisdom yet for none."—*Bayard Taylor.*

"To know
That which before us lies in daily life,
Is the prime wisdom."—*Milton.*

Show that this is true from the following or other stories of the Bible: Examples: I. Kings iii. 5–16; II. Chronicles i.; Job xxxiii.

1. Cause me to know the way wherein I should walk; for I lift up my soul unto thee. Teach me to do thy will; for thou art my God; thy spirit is good; lead me into the land of uprightness. (Psalms cxliii. 8–10.)

2. Teach me thy way, O Lord; I will walk in thy truth; unite my heart to fear thy name. (Psalms lxxxvi. 11.)

3. He that trusteth in his own heart is a fool; but whoso walketh wisely, he shall be delivered. (Proverbs xxviii. 26.)

4. Woe unto them that are wise in their own eyes, and prudent in their own sight. (Isaiah v. 21.)

5. If thou be wise, thou shalt be wise for thyself; but if thou scornest, thou alone shalt bear it. (Proverbs ix. 12.)

6. Through wisdom is a house built; and by understanding it is established; and by knowledge shall the chambers be filled with all precious and pleasant riches. (Proverbs xxiv. 3–4.)

7. Hear counsel, and receive instructions, that thou mayest be wise in thy latter end. (Proverbs xix. 20.)

8. My son, forget not my law; but let thy heart keep my commandments. For length of days, and long life, and peace, shall they add to thee. Let not mercy and truth forsake thee; bind them about thy neck; write them upon the table of thy heart. So shalt thou find favor and good understanding in the sight of God and man. (Proverbs iii. 1–4.)

9. A scorner loveth not one that reproveth him; neither will he go unto the wise. (Proverbs xv. 12.)

C.—DUTIES IN GENERAL.

I.—DUTIES OF PARENTS TO CHILDREN.

It is the duty of parents to afford to their children a good example in all things by their own conduct in life. Parents must do all they can to provide for their children and make their homes the dearest spot on earth. The Rabbis laid down the rule that every parent must train the body, mind and soul of his child, must teach him to exercise his body and learn a trade, but, "the study of the law," which means the training of the mind and spirit, this "exceeds all things."

"The effect of precept is slow and tedious, that of example is quick and effectual."—*Seneca.*

"Do not train children to learning by force and harshness; but direct them to it by what amuses their minds, so that you may be the better able to discover with accuracy the peculiar bent of the genius of each."—*Plato.*

"Delightful task! to rear the tender thought,
To teach the young idea how to shoot,
To pour the fresh instruction o'er the mind,
To breathe the enlivening spirit, and to fix
The generous purpose in the glowing breast."—*Thomson.*

1. And these words, which I command thee this day, shall be in thy heart; and thou shalt teach them diligently unto thy children, and thou shalt talk of them when thou sittest in thy house, and when thou walkest by the way, and when thou liest down, and when thou risest up. (Deuteronomy vi. 6-7.)

2. Gather me the people together, and I will make them hear my words, that they may learn to fear me all the days that they shall live upon the earth, and that they may teach their children. (Deuteronomy iv. 10.)

3. Train up a child in the way he should go, and when he is old he will not depart from it. (Proverbs xxii. 6.)

4. Correct thy son, and he shall give thee rest; yea, he shall give delight unto thy soul. (Proverbs xxix. 17.)

5. Seeing that Abraham shall become a great and mighty nation, and all the nations of the earth shall be blessed in him, for I know him, that he will command his children and his household after him, and they shall keep the way of the Lord, to do justice and judgment; that the Lord may bring upon Abraham that which he hath spoken of him. (Genesis xviii. 18-19.)

6. Withhold not correction from the child, for if thou beatest him with the rod, he shall not die. Thou shalt beat him with a rod and shall deliver his soul from destruction. (Proverbs xxiii. 13-14.)

7. Foolishness is bound in the heart of a child; but the rod of correction shall drive it far from him. (Proverbs xxii. 15.)

8. He that spareth his rod hateth his son, but he that loveth him, chastiseth him betimes. (Proverbs xiii. 24.)

II.—DUTIES OF CHILDREN TO THEIR PARENTS.

"Honor thy father and thy mother," is the command that contains all our duties to our parents. There are many ways in which we may honor our parents; but the first is by obeying them in everything, no matter how small or great, unless it is something wrong. There are many little things in which we can show honor, respect and love to our parents every day. Our Rabbis give some of these, as: "Do not vex them, nor disturb their sleep. Do not sit down in their place. Do not deny what they say, nor agree with their words in such a way as to seem to decide whether they are right or wrong. Speak to them and of them only in the most respectful terms."

"The dutifulness of children is the foundation of all virtues."—*Cicero*.

Examples: Genesis xxxvii. 29–36; II. Samuel xv. 1–15; II. Samuel xviii. 1–16; II. Samuel xviii. 28–32; Genesis xxii. 1–14; Genesis xliv. 18–34; Genesis xlv. 1–14; I. Kings xix. 19–20.

1. Children's children are the crown of old men; and the glory of children are their fathers. (Proverbs xvii. 6.)
2. Behold, how good and how pleasant it is for brethren to dwell together in unity. (Psalms cxxxiii. 1.)
3. My son, hear the instructions of thy father, and forsake not the law of thy mother. (Proverbs i. 8.)
4. Ye shall fear every man his mother and his father, and keep my Sabbaths; I am the Lord your God. (Leviticus xix. 3.)
5. Hearken unto thy father that begat thee, and despise not thy mother when she is old. Buy the truth and sell it not; also wisdom and instruction and understanding. The father of the righteous shall greatly rejoice; and he that begetteth a wise child shall have joy of him. (Proverbs xxxiii. 22–24.)
6. A wise son maketh a glad father; but a foolish son is the heaviness of his mother. (Proverbs x. 1.)
7. A foolish son is a grief to his father and bitterness to her that bore him. (Proverbs xvii. 25.)
8. The rod and reproof give wisdom; but a child left to himself bringeth his mother to shame. (Proverbs xxix. 15.)
9. Whoso keepeth the law is a wise son; but he that is a companion of riotous men shameth his father. (Proverbs xxviii. 7.)
10. Whoso robbeth his father or his mother, and saith, "It is no transgression"; the same is the companion of a destroyer. (Proverbs xxviii. 24.)
11. He that plundereth his father and chaseth away his mother, is a son that causeth shame and bringeth reproach. (Proverbs xix. 26.)
12. The eye that mocketh at his father and despiseth to obey his mother, the ravens of the valley shall pick it out, and the young eagles shall eat it. (Proverbs xxx. 17.)

13. Whoso curseth his father or his mother his lamp shall be put out in obscure darkness. (Proverbs xx. 20.)

14. Cursed be he that speaketh lightly of his father or mother, and all the people shall say, Amen. (Deuteronomy xxvii. 16.)

III.—DUTIES OF MASTER AND SERVANT.

In telling what the duties of a master are, Rabbi Moses ben Maimon said: "The master shall not distress his servant nor harm him; shall put no heavy burden upon him; but, on the contrary, shall care for him properly, and feed and clothe him well. He must not give his orders in a loud and scolding tone, but be calm and patient, and listen to what the servant has to say." Prompt obedience, strict honesty, and a careful doing of all his duties are required of the servant.

Show the truth of the foregoing by the following or other stories of the Bible: Examples: Genesis xxiv.; II. Samuel xv. 18–23.

---

1. Thou shalt not oppress a hired servant that is poor and needy, whether he be of thy brethren, or of thy strangers that are in thy land within thy gates: at his day thou shalt give him his hire, neither shall the sun go down upon it; for he is poor and setteth his heart upon it; lest he cry against thee unto the Lord, and it be sin unto thee. (Deuteronomy xxiv. 14–15.)

2. The wages of him that is hired shall not abide with thee all night until the morning. (Leviticus xix. 13.)

3. Woe unto him that buildeth his house by unrighteousness, and his chambers by wrong; that useth his neighbor's service without wages, and giveth him nought for his work. (Jeremiah xxii. 13.)

4. And if thy brother that dwelleth by thee be waxen poor, and be sold unto thee, thou shalt not compel him to serve as a bond-servant, but as a hired servant, and as a sojourner he shall be with thee, and shall serve thee unto the year of jubilee. Thou shalt not rule

over him with rigor; but shalt fear thy God. (Leviticus xxv. 39-40, 43.)

5. And when thou sendest him out free from thee, thou shalt not let him go away empty; thou shalt furnish him liberally out of thy flock, and out of thy floor, and out of thy wine-press, of that wherewith the Lord thy God hath blessed thee thou shalt give unto him, and thou shalt remember that thou wast a bondsman in the land of Egypt and the Lord thy God redeemed thee; therefore, I command thee this thing to-day. (Deuteronomy xv. 13-15.)

6. Whoso keepeth the fig tree shall eat the fruit thereof; so he that waiteth on his master shall be honored. (Proverbs xxvii. 18.)

IV.—DUTIES TO OUR BENEFACTORS.

It is our duty to be thankful for every kindness, great or small, that is shown to us. We must never forget the same, but must know how to appreciate it and must eagerly strive to repay it at least with equal kindness.

Our greatest benefactors are our parents and teachers, and all those who labor to bring us up and educate us and help us along. We never can do enough to thank them for their care and patience and kindness, but by our noble conduct we may best prove to them that we really value their good acts.

"That man is worthless who knows how to receive a favor, but not how to return one."—*Plautus.*

"There is no benefit so small that a good man will not magnify it."
—*Seneca.*

"A thankful heart is not only the greatest virtue, but the parent of all other virtues."—*Cicero.*

"Let the man who would be grateful think of repaying a kindness, even while receiving it."—*Seneca.*

"Earth produces nothing worse than an ungrateful man."—*Ansonius*.

1. Whoso bestoweth evil in return for good, evil shall not depart from his house. (Proverbs xvii. 13.)
2. They also that repay me evil in lieu of good; they hate me bitterly because I pursue what is good. (Psalms xxxviii. 21.)
3. Shall evil be recompensed instead of good, that they have dug a pit against my life? (Jeremiah xviii. 20.)

V.—DUTIES TOWARD ORPHANS, WIDOWS, STRANGERS, OR THOSE OF OTHER BELIEFS.

Sad is the lot of the homeless, the widow and the orphan, who are forced to depend on the kindness of strangers. It is our duty to open our hearts to all such, it makes no difference who they are, or of what religion they may be, for we are all the children of one Heavenly Father.

We must not treat them with unjust suspicion or take any advantage of them, but rather look upon them as belonging to us, as equals, and treat them so, doing nothing to them that we should hate to have done to us.

Examples: Genesis xviii. 1–9; Ruth ii. 2–19; I. Samuel xx.; Genesis xxiii.; Genesis xl.

1. The Lord guardeth the strangers; the fatherless and widow he helpeth up (Psalms cxlvi. 9.)
2. For the Lord your God is the God of gods, and the Lord of lords, the great, the mighty and the terrible God, who hath no regard for persons and taketh no bribe. Who executeth justice for the fatherless and the widow, and loveth the stranger to give him food and raiment. Love ye then the stranger; for you have been strangers in the land of Egypt. (Deuteronomy x. 17–19.)

3. When thou hast made an end of giving away all the tithe in the third year, the year of the tithing, and hast given it unto the Levite, to the stranger, to the fatherless, and to the widow, and they have eaten within thy gates, and are satisfied. (Deuteronomy xxvi. 12.)

4. As a bird that wandereth away from its nest, so is a man that wandereth away from his place. (Proverbs xxvii. 8.)

5. Weep not for the dead, and do not bemoan him; weep sorely for him that goeth away; for he shall never return any more and see the land of his birth. (Jeremiah xxii. 10.)

6. And if a stranger sojourn with thee in your land, ye shall not vex him. As one born in the land among you, shall be unto you the stranger that sojourneth with you, and thou shalt love him as thyself; for ye were strangers in the land of Egypt. I am the Lord your God. (Leviticus xix. 33-34.)

7. And a stranger thou shalt not vex, and shalt not oppress him; for strangers ye were in the land of Egypt. (Exodus xxii. 20.)

8. And a stranger shalt thou not oppress; for ye know well the spirit of the stranger, seeing ye yourselves were strangers in the land of Egypt. (Exodus xxiii. 9.)

9. Cursed be he that perverteth the cause of the stranger, of the fatherless and the widow; and all the people shall say, Amen. (Deuteronomy xxvii. 19.)

10. Congregation! one statute shall be for you and for the stranger that sojourneth; a statute forever in your generations; as ye are, so shall the stranger be before the Lord. One law and one code shall be for you and for the stranger that sojourneth with you. (Numbers xv. 15-16.)

VI.—OUR DUTIES TOWARD OUR COUNTRY.

Those who rule a country must ever be faithful in doing their duty, must serve for the good of the people, and not for their own profit; must be honest, just and merciful. Therefore, we should be very

DUTIES IN GENERAL.

careful in selecting officers, not to let anything influence us to choose any but those who are upright and able.

The people must obey the law, and peaceably submit to the rulers. If these be cruel and unjust, they must be patient, for justice is from God and will surely come.

"Let the interest of the place in which you dwell be your own," said one of our great Rabbis, and so, indeed, we should serve our country with all our power and wealth, and not hesitate to fight for it and lay down our lives in its behalf.

"Let all the ends thou aim'st at be thy country's, thy God's and truth's." —*Shakespeare.*

"I do love my country's good with a respect more tender, more holy and profound than mine own life."—*Shakespeare.*

"This nation, under God, shall have a new birth of freedom, and that government of the people, by the people, for the people, shall not perish from the earth."—*Lincoln.*

"Of all human things nothing is more honorable, or more excellent, than to deserve well of one's country."—*Cicero.*

"How sleep the brave, who sink to rest,
By all their country's wishes blest."—*Collins.*

Prove that the above is true by the following or other stories in the Bible: Examples: I. Samuel viii.; Judges iv., vi., xi.; I. Samuel xvii. 20–58; I. Samuel xii.; Joshua vi., vii.; Numbers xiii., xiv.

---

1. Even in thy thought thou must not curse a king; and in thy bedchambers do not curse the rich; for a bird of the air can carry the sound, and that which hath wings can tell the word. (Ecclesiastes x. 20.)

2. My son, fear the Lord and the king; with those that are desirous to change, do not mingle thyself. (Proverbs xxiv. 21.)

3. The judges thou shalt not revile; and a ruler among thy people thou shalt not curse. (Exodus xxii. 27.)

4. And seek the welfare of the city, whither I have banished you, and pray in its behalf unto the Lord, for in its welfare shall ye fare well. (Jeremiah xxix. 7.)

5. Kindness and truth will watch over a king, and he will prop up through kindness his throne. (Proverbs xx. 28.)

6. When a king judgeth in truth the indigent, his throne shall stand firmly forever. (Proverbs xxix. 14.)

7. There should be a wise sentence on the lips of the king, his mouth should never commit a trespass in judging. It should be an abomination to kings to commit wickedness, for through righteousness (alone) can a throne be established. Righteous lips (should obtain) the favor of kings, and him that speaketh uprightly should they love. The fury of a king is like the messenger of death; but a wise man will appease it. (Proverbs xvi. 10, 12–14.)

8. If a ruler listen to the word of falsehood, all his servants become wicked. (Proverbs xxix. 12.)

9. A king will, through the exercise of justice, establish (the welfare of) a land; but one that loveth gifts overthroweth it. (Proverbs xxix. 4.)

10. Not for kings, oh, Lemoel! (not for kings) is it fitting to drink wine, nor for princes strong drink. Lest either might drink and forget what is written in the law, and pervert the cause of all the afflicted. Give strong drink unto him that is ready to perish, and wine unto those who have an imbittered soul. Let such a one drink and forget his poverty and remember his trouble no more. Open thy mouth for the dumb, for the cause of all fatherless children. Open thy mouth, judge righteously, and decide the cause of the poor and needy. (Proverbs xxxi. 4–9.)

11. And he appointed judges in the land, in all the fortified cities of Judah; in city by city, and he said to the judges, "Look (well) at what ye are doing; because not for man are ye to judge, but for the Lord, who is with you in pronouncing judgment. And now let

the dread of the Lord be upon you; take heed and act; for with the Lord, our God, there is no injustice, nor respect for persons, nor taking of bribes." (II. Chronicles xix. 5 7.)

12. Many seek the favor of a ruler, but from the Lord cometh justice for man. (Proverbs xxix. 26.)

VII.—OUR DUTIES TOWARD THE AGED AND HELPLESS.

Those who are unhappy in not having the use of their bodily powers, such as the aged, the blind, the deaf, the dumb, and the lame, these should have our sympathy and aid. None should laugh at or mock them, but rather pity and try to serve them. Great is the joy we can bring to the hearts of those who are helpless, and it is so easy to do this, and make our own hearts feel so much lighter and nobler, that we should never neglect to fulfill this simple duty.

Show the truth of the foregoing by the following or other stories in the Bible: Examples: I. Kings xii.; Job xxxii. 4-7; Genesis xiv. 8-24; Exodus ii. 1-20; II. Samuel ix.

1. Happy is he that careth for the poor; on the day of evil will the Lord deliver him. (Psalms xli. 2)

2. Whoso stoppeth his ears against the cry of the poor, he also will cry himself, but shall not be answered. (Proverbs xxi. 13.)

3. Whoso mocketh the poor, blasphemeth his Maker; he that is glad at calamities will not remain unpunished. (Proverbs xvii. 5.)

4. He that oppresseth the poor, blasphemeth his Maker, but he that is gracious to the needy honoreth him. (Proverbs xiv. 31.)

5. Rob not the poor, because he is poor, neither crush the afflicted in the gate. For the Lord will plead their cause, and despoil the life of those that despoil them. (Proverbs xxii. 22-23)

6. Remove not the ancient land-mark, and in the fields of the

fatherless must thou not enter. For their redeemer is strong ; he will indeed plead their cause with thee. (Proverbs xxiii. 10-11.)

7. God standeth in the congregation of God; in the midst of judges does he judge. How long will ye judge unjustly, and treat with favor the face of the wicked? Judge uprightly the poor and the fatherless; do justice to the afflicted and indigent. Release the poor and needy, deliver them out of the power of the wicked. They know not, nor will they understand, in darkness do they walk on; all the foundations of the earth are moved. I have, indeed, said, "Ye are God's; and children of the Most High are all of you." But, verily, like men shall ye die, and like one of the princes shall ye fall. Arise, O God, judge the earth; for thou wilt possess all the nations. (Psalms lxxxii.)

8. Thou shalt not curse the deaf, nor put a stumbling-block before the blind; but thou shalt be afraid of thy God: I am the Lord. (Leviticus xix. 14.)

9. Cursed be he that causeth the blind to wander out of the way, and all the people shall say, Amen. (Deuteronomy xxvii. 18.)

10. Before the hoary head shalt thou rise up, and honor the face of the old man; and thou shalt be afraid of thy God: I am the Lord. (Leviticus xix. 32.)

VIII.—OUR DUTIES TOWARD THE LOWER ANIMALS.

No creature which God has created should be thoughtlessly injured or abused. The feelings of animals should be cared for not less than those of men, and any cruelty toward them is a crime.

No beast of burden should be overladen or overworked, and none should be beaten. Proper food and rest are as needful for animals as for man.

Prove that the above is true by the following or other stories in the Bible: Example: Jonah iv. 11.

1. Thy righteousness is like the great mountains, thy judgments are a great deep: O Lord, thou preservest man and beast. (Psalms xxxvi. 7.)

2. Six days shalt thou do thy work, and on the seventh day shalt thou rest; that thy ox and thy ass may repose, and the son of thy hand-maid, and the stranger may be refreshed. (Exodus xxiii. 12.)

3. And (the product of) the Sabbath of the land shall be unto you for food, for thee, and for thy man-servant, and for thy maid-servant, and for thy hired laborer, and for thy stranger that sojourneth with thee, and for thy cattle, and for the beasts that are in thy land, shall all its products be (left) for food. (Leviticus xxv. 6–7.)

4. A righteous man careth for the life of his beast; but the mercies of the wicked are cruelty. (Proverbs xii. 10.)

5. Thou shalt not see thy brother's ass, or his ox fallen down by the way, and withdraw thyself from them; thou shalt surely help him to lift them up again. (Deuteronomy xxii. 4.)

6. Thou shalt not plow with an ox and an ass together. (Deuteronomy xxii. 10.)

7. Thou shalt not muzzle the ox when he thresheth out the corn. (Deuteronomy xxv. 4.)

8. If a bird's nest chance to be before thee in the way, on any tree, or on the ground with young ones, or with eggs, and the mother be sitting upon the young, or upon the eggs; thou shalt not take the mother with the young. (Deuteronomy xxii. 6.)

D.—OUR RELIGIOUS DUTIES.

I.—BE EVER MINDFUL OF THE COMMANDMENTS OF GOD AND ACT UP TO THEM.

Some form of religion is found in every part of the world and among all peoples, for the feeling that gives us faith in a God and makes us long to become purer and more perfect is in every human heart. This feeling it is our duty to strengthen and cultivate; in the Bible we may find the means of doing this, that is, in the commandments of God. To know and understand them is our great duty, but we must remember that "it is the *doing*, not the *knowing*, which is the principal thing," as one of our Rabbis said.

"Without religion whither will ye flee for safety in a world full of death, full of warring passions?

"Envy with its companions, slander and malice, assail you in every direction, so soon as ye begin to take comfort in it, so soon as you become in any way to distinguish yourself in it. Wherever ye flee injustice and wickedness are the stronger. Neither are you true to yourself; no inclination, no purpose, no living and strengthening thought can ye hold fast at will. Perfect blessedness is nowhere, and nowhere would there be consolation even, if religion were not. Religion alone can purify life."—*Jacobi.*

---

1. Wherewithal shall a youth keep his way pure? By guiding it according to thy word. (Psalms cxix. 9.)
2. Depart from evil and do good; seek peace and pursue it. (Psalms xxxiv. 15.)
3. This day the Lord thy God commandeth thee to do these statutes and ordinances; and thou shalt keep and do them with all thy heart, and with all thy soul. (Deuteronomy xxvi. 16.)
4. The Lord will raise thee up unto himself as a holy people, as

he hath sworn unto thee; if thou wilt keep the commandments of the Lord thy God and walk in his ways. (Deuteronomy xxviii. 9.)

5. For this commandment which I command thee this day, is not hidden from thee, nor is it far off. It is not in heaven, that thou shouldst say, "Who will go up for us to heaven, and fetch it down unto us, and cause us to hear it, that we may do it?" Neither is it beyond the sea, that thou shouldst say, "Who will go over the sea for us and fetch it unto us, and cause us to hear it, that we may do it?" But the word is very nigh unto thee, in thy mouth and in thy heart, that thou mayest do it. (Deuteronomy xxx. 11-14.)

6. Happy are those that observe justice, that execute righteousness at all times. (Psalms cvi. 3.)

II.—BE FILLED WITH AWE BEFORE GOD, THAT YOU MAY DO NO WRONG.

Every one of us, no doubt, knows some person whom we believe to be good and noble, and out of regard for whom we would not allow ourselves to do or say the least wrong thing. How much more should we stand in awe of God, who is perfect, and whose wonderful works as we see them within us and in the world about us, fill us with that sublime religious feeling which is called in the Bible "the fear of God." That feeling makes us love him, and long to become perfect like him, it makes us worship him, makes us obedient to his holy will, it keeps us pure and elevates our spiritual nature.

> "Acquaint thyself with God if thou wouldst taste
> His works; admitted once to his embrace,
> Thou shalt perceive that thou wert blind before.
> Thine eye shalt be instructed, and thine heart
> Made pure shall relish, with divine delight
> Till then unfelt, what hands divine hath wrought."—*Cowper.*

> "A God alone can comprehend a God."—*Young.*

BIBLE ETHICS.

"Live with men as if God saw you."—*Seneca.*

Prove that the above is true by the following or other stories in the Bible: Example: I. Chronicles xxviii.

1. Come ye children, hearken unto me; the fear of the Lord will I teach you. (Psalms xxxiv. 12.)

2. Do now hear this, O sottish people, who have no heart; who have eyes, and see not; who have ears, and hear not. Will ye not fear me? saith the Lord; will ye not tremble at my presence, who have placed the sand as a bound for the sea by an everlasting law, which it can never pass over? And though the waves thereof be upheaved, yet can they not prevail, though they roar, yet can they not pass over it. But this people hath a stubborn and a rebellious heart; they have departed (from the right) and have gone their way. And they have not said in their heart, "Let us now fear the Lord our God, that giveth rain, the early and the latter rain in its season; the appointed weeks of the harvest doth he ever preserve for us." (Jeremiah v. 21-24.)

3. Who would not fear thee, O King of the nations? for to thee doth it appertain; because among all the wise men of the nations and in all their kingdoms (they say) there is none like unto thee. (Jeremiah x. 7.)

4. Only fear the Lord and serve him in truth with all your heart; for see what great things he hath done with you. (I. Samuel xii. 24.)

5. And now, Israel, what doth the Lord thy God require of thee, but to fear the Lord thy God, to walk in all his ways, and to love him and to serve the Lord thy God with all thy heart and with all thy soul, to keep the commandments of the Lord and his statutes, which I command thee this day for thine own good? Behold, to the Lord thy God belong the heavens and the heavens of heavens, and the earth with all that is thereon. (Deuteronomy x. 12-14.)

6. A son honoreth his father and a servant his master; if then I be a father, where is my honor, and if I be a master where is the fear of me? saith the Lord of hosts. (Malachi i. 6.)

OUR RELIGIOUS DUTIES.

7. Fear not; for in order to prove you, did God come, and in order that his fear may be before your faces, that ye sin not. (Exodus xx. 17.)

8. Happy is the man that feareth the Lord, that greatly delighteth in his commandments. (Psalms cxii. 1.)

9. The fear of the Lord increaseth (man's) days; but the years of the wicked shall be shortened. (Proverbs x. 27.)

10. When I call on the name of the Lord, ascribe ye greatness unto our God. (Deuteronomy xxxii. 3.)

11. Suffer not thy heart to be rash, and let thy heart not be hasty to utter any word before God; for God is in the heavens and thou art upon the earth; therefore, let thy words be few. (Ecclesiastes v. 1.)

12. The Lord thy God shalt thou fear; him shalt thou serve, and to him shalt thou clevae, and by his name shalt thou swear. (Deuteronomy x. 20.)

13. And if thou wilt swear, As the Lord liveth, in truth, in justice and in righteousness, then shall nations bless themselves in him, and in him shall they glorify themselves. (Jeremiah iv. 2.)

14. And ye shall not swear by my name falsely, and thou shalt not thus profane the name of thy God; I am the Lord. (Leviticus xix. 12.)

15. And I will come near unto you to (hold) judgment; and I will be a swift witness against the sorcerers, and against the adulterers, and against those that swear falsely, and against those that withhold the wages of the hired laborer, (oppress) the widow and the fatherless, and that do injustice to the stranger, and who fear me not, saith the Lord of hosts. (Malachi iii. 5.)

16. Then conversed they that fear the Lord one with the other; and the Lord listened and heard it, and there was written a book of remembrance before him for those who fear the Lord and for those who respect his name. (Malachi iii. 16.)

17. Who shall ascend unto the mountain of the Lord? and who shall be able to stand in his holy place? He that is clean of hands and pure of heart; who hath not lifted up his soul unto falsehood and

hath not sworn deceitfully. He shall bear away blessing from the Lord, and (the reward of) righteousness from the God of his salvation. (Psalms xxiv. 3-5.)

III.—THOU SHALT LOVE GOD THY LORD WITH ALL THY HEART.

The first feelings of love are awakened in our hearts by the kindness, the gentleness and love of those who are so tireless and patient in taking care of us. As we grow older and can use our minds in directing the feelings of our hearts, it is toward that which is true and beautiful in character and in grace that we are drawn. How much more then should we be drawn in love toward God, who is our ideal of perfection in kindness, power and holiness.

"Thou, my all!
My theme, my inspiration, and my crown!
My strength in age, my rise in low estate!
My soul's ambition, pleasure, wealth! My world,
My light in darkness! and my life in death!
My boast through time! bliss through eternity!
Eternity, too short to speak thy praise!
Or fathom thy profound love to man."—*Young.*

1. And thou shalt love the Lord thy God with all thy heart and with all thy soul and with all thy might. (Deuteronomy vi. 5.)

2. Take good heed, therefore, for your soul's sake, to love the Lord your God. (Joshua xxiii. 11.)

3. Thou shalt, therefore, love the Lord thy God, and keep his charge, and his statutes, and his ordinances, and his commandments all the days. (Deuteronomy xi. 1.)

4. For if ye will diligently keep all this commandment which I command you, in order to do it, to love the Lord your God, to walk in all his ways and to cleave unto him. (Deuteronomy xi. 22.)

5. In that I command thee this day to love the Lord thy God, to walk in his ways and to keep his commandments and his statutes and his ordinances, that thou mayest live and multiply; and that the Lord thy God will bless thee in the lands whither thou goest to possess it. (Deuteronomy xxx. 16.)

6. To love the Lord thy God, to hearken to his voice and to cleave unto him; for he is thy life and the length of thy days. (Deuteronomy xxx. 20)

IV.—BE THANKFUL FOR ALL OF GOD'S GOODNESS.

The world is full of wonderful things in which we find healing for our pains, satisfaction for our hunger and thirst, pleasures for our senses, and untold delights for the heart. All these things should fill us with a deep gratitude to the great giver—God. We can do nothing to repay him for all his kindness; all we can do is to try and be worthy of it.

We despise the man who is ungrateful for any kindness shown to him, how much more is he to be despised who fails to thank his Maker.

Let us rejoice and be glad in God's goodness and bring thanks to him with full and joyous hearts, in prayer, in praise and in song.

"Whatever will make us better, happier, God has placed either openly before us or very close to us."—*Seneca.*

"Let us never day nor night unhallowed pass,
But still remember what the Lord hath done."—*Shakespeare.*

"Thank God for rest,
Where none molest,
And none can make afraid;
For Peace that sits
As Plenty's guest
Beneath the homestead's shade."

Prove that the above is true by the following or other stories in the Bible: Examples: I. Samuel i., ii.; I. Samuel xii.; II. Samuel xxii.

---

1. I am not worthy of all the kindness and of all the truth which thou hast shown unto thy servant. (Genesis xxxii. 11.)

2. What shall I give in return unto the Lord for all his bounties toward me? (Psalms cxvi. 12.)

3. They (therefore) shall give thanks unto the Lord for his kindness, and (proclaim) his wonders to the children of men! For he satisfied the longing soul, and the hungry soul he filled with good. (Psalms cvii. 8–9.)

4. When thou hast eaten and art satisfied, then shalt thou bless the Lord thy God for the good land which he hath given thee. (Deuteronomy viii. 10.)

5. Take heed unto thyself that thou forget not the Lord thy God, so as not to keep his commandments, and his ordinances, and his statutes, which I command thee this day; that when thou hast eaten and art satisfied and hast built goodly houses, and dwelt therein; and when thy herds and thy flocks multiply, and thy silver and thy gold are multiplied, and all that thou hast is multiplied: Thy heart be then not lifted up, and thou forget the Lord thy God who hath brought thee forth out of the land of Egypt, from the house of slavery; who hath led thee through the great and terrible wilderness, wherein are snakes, poisonous serpents and scorpions, and drought, where there is no water; who hath brought forth for thee water out of the flinty rock; who hath fed thee in the wilderness with manna, which thy fathers knew not; in order to afflict thee, and in order to prove thee, to do thee good at thy latter end; and thou say in thy heart, "My power and the strength of my hand have gotten me this wealth." But thou shalt remember the Lord thy God; for it is he that giveth thee power to get wealth; in order that he might fulfill his covenant which he hath sworn unto thy fathers, as it is this day. (Deuteronomy viii. 11–18.)

6. Will ye thus requite the Lord, O people, worthless and unwise? Is he not thy father who hath bought thee? Is it not he who hath made thee, and established thee? (Deuteronomy xxxii. 6.)

7. I will thank thee with uprightness of heart, when I learn thy righteous ordinances. (Psalms cxix. 7.)

8. It is a good thing to give thanks unto the Lord and to sing praises unto thy name, O Most High! To tell in the morning of thy kindness and of thy faithfulness in the nights. (Psalms xcii. 2–3.)

9. Hallelujah! Praise, O my soul, the Lord. I will praise the Lord throughout my life; I will sing praises unto my God while I have any being. (Psalms cxlvi. 1–2.)

10. But as for us, we will bless the Lord from this time forth and for evermore. Hallelujah! (Psalms cxv. 18.)

11. But verily God hath heard: he hath listened to the voice of my prayer. Blessed be God who hath not removed my prayer (from him) nor his kindness from me. (Psalms lxvi. 19–20.)

12. Blessed be the Lord, because he hath heard the voice of my supplications. The Lord is my strength and my shield; in him hath my heart trusted, and I am helped, and my heart exulteth; and with my song will I thank him. (Psalms xxviii. 6-7.)

13. I will praise the name of God with song, and will magnify him with thanksgiving. And this will please the Lord better than an ox or bullock having horns and cloven hoofs. The meek will see this and be rejoiced; ye that seek God, and your heart shall rejoice. For the Lord listeneth unto the needy, and his prisoners he despiseth not. Let heaven and earth praise him, the seas, and everything that moveth therein. (Psalms lxix. 31–35.)

14. All thy works shall thank thee, O Lord, and thy pious servants shall bless thee. (Psalms cxlv. 10.)

15. Hallelujah; for the Lord is good; sing praises unto his holy name; for it is lovely. For Jacob hath the Lord chosen unto himself, Israel, as his peculiar treasure. (Psalms cxxxv. 3-4.)

16. A song of the degrees by David. If it had not been the Lord who was for us, so should Israel say; if it had not been the Lord who

was for us, when men rose up against us; then would they have swallowed us up alive when their wrath was kindled against us; then would the waters have overwhelmed us, the stream would have passed over our soul. Then would have passed over our soul the presumptuous waters. Bless the Lord who hath not given us up as a prey to their teeth. Our soul is escaped like the bird out of the snare of the fowlers; the snare is broken and we are escaped. Our help is in the name of the Lord, the maker of heaven and earth. (Psalms cxxiv.)

17. A psalm of thanksgiving. Shout joyfully unto the Lord all ye ands. Serve the Lord with joy; come before his presence with triumphal song. Know that the Lord is God indeed; it is he that hath made us, and his are we—his people and the flock of his pasture. Enter his gates with thanksgiving, his courts with praise; give thanks unto him, bless his name. For the Lord is good, to eternity endureth his kindness and unto the latest generation his truth. (Psalms c.)

V.—TRUST FIRMLY IN GOD AND BOW WITH PIOUS HUMILITY TO HIS WILL.

Although man has been created in the image of God, although he has been gifted with reason and judgment, still he is but a mortal. His knowledge is limited, it can not reach beyond the sphere which has been assigned to him. Everywhere we are surrounded by mysteries and wonders, before which we stand in awe.

Oftentimes we are afflicted with troubles and suffering, which in our shortsightedness we regard as unjust. But whatever of evil happens to us we must humbly submit to it. "The mysteries and secret things belong to the Eternal, our God." God's wisdom is beyond our comprehension. What we regard as wrong often turns out to be of great benefit. God strikes, but he also heals, and in his healing there is more of Divine blessing than there has been evil in his strokes.

OUR RELIGIOUS DUTIES.

"Oh, deem not they are blest alone,
Whose lives a peaceful tenor keep!
The power who pities man hath shown,
A blessing for the eyes that weep.

"The light of smiles shall fill again,
The lids that overflow with tears,
And weary hours of woe and pain,
Are promises of happier years."—*William Cullen Bryant.*

"God shall be my hope,
My stay, my guide and lantern to my feet."—*Shakespeare.*

"The good are better made by ill,
As odors crushed are sweeter still."—*Rogers.*

"The path of sorrow, and that path alone,
Leads to the land where sorrow is unknown."—*Cowper.*

"Nor let the good man's trust depart,
Though life its common gifts deny,
Though with a pierced and bleeding heart,
And spurned of man, he goes to die.

"For God hath marked each sorrowing day,
And numbered every sacred tear,
And Heaven's long age of bliss shall pay
For all his children suffers here."
—*William Cullen Bryant.*

Prove that the above are true by the following or other stories in the Bible: Examples: II. Samuel xii. 16-23; II. Chronicles xxxii. 1-27; Job iv., xiii.

---

1. That thy trust may be in the Lord, have I made them known to thee this day, yea, even to thee. (Proverbs xxii. 19.)
2. He giveth to the faint strength; and to the powerless he imparteth much might.
Though youths should grow faint and be weary, and young men should utterly stumble:
Yet they that wait upon the Lord shall acquire new strength, they

shall mount up with wings as eagles; they shall run and not be weary, they shall walk and not become faint. (Isaiah xl. 29-31.)

3. The Lord is my rock, and my fortress, and my deliverer; my God, my rock, in whom I trust; my shield and the horn of my salvation, and my high tower. (Psalms xviii. 3.)

4. For thou wilt cause my light to shine; the Lord my God will enlighten my darkness.

For (aided) by thee I run through a troop; and (helped) by my God I leap over a wall. As for God his way is perfect; the word of the Lord is tried; he is a shield to all those that trust in him. (Psalms xviii. 29-31.)

5. But the Lord will sit enthroned forever; he hath established forgiving judgment his throne.

And he will judge the world with righteousness, he shall decide for the people with equity.

The Lord also will be a stronghold for the oppressed, a stronghold in times of distress. And they that know thy name will put their trust in thee; for thou hast not forsaken those that seek thee, O Lord! (Psalms ix. 8-11.)

6. Unto thee, O Lord, do I lift up my soul. O my God, in thee do I trust, let me not be ashamed, let not mine enemies triumph over me.

Yea, none that wait on thee will be put to shame: let those be put to shame who deal treacherously without cause. Show me, O Lord, thy ways; teach me thy paths.

Lead me in thy truth, and teach me; for thou art the God of my salvation; on thee do I wait all the day. (Psalms xxv. 1-5.)

7. It is good for a man that he bear the yoke in his youth;

That he sit in solitude and be silent; because he hath laid it upon him;

That he put his mouth in the dust; perhaps there still is hope;

That he offer his cheek to him that smiteth him; that he be satisfied with reproach;

For the Lord will not cast off forever;

But though he have caused grief, yet will he have mercy, according to the abundance of his kindness. (Lamentations iii. 27-32.)

8. For thus hath said the Lord Eternal, the Holy One of Israel, In repose and rest shall ye be helped; in quietness and in confidence shall be your strength. (Isaiah xxx. 15.)

9. And Moses said unto the people, "Fear ye not, stand still, and see the salvation of the Lord, which he will do for you to-day; for as ye have seen the Egyptians to-day, ye shall not see them again any more forever. The Lord shall fight for you and you shall hold your peace." (Exodus xiv. 13, 14.)

10. He is the Lord; let him do what seemeth good in his eyes. (I. Samuel iii. 18.)

11. And the King said unto Zadok, "Carry back the ark of God into the city; if I shall find favor in the eyes of the Lord, he will bring me back again, and show me both it and his dwelling.

But if he should thus say, I have no delight in thee; here am I, let him do to me as seemeth good in his eyes." (II. Samuel xv. 25, 26.)

The Lord gave, and the Lord hath taken away, may the name of the Lord be blessed. (Job i. 21.)

13. The Lord is my light and my salvation, of whom shall I be afraid? The Lord is the fortress of my life, of whom shall I have dread? (Psalms xxvii. 1.)

14. And the Lord it is that goeth before thee; he will be with thee, he will not let thee fail, nor will he forsake thee: fear not, nor be thou discouraged. (Deuteronomy xxxi. 8.)

15. God is our protection and strength, a help in distresses very readily found. Therefore, will ye not fear, even when the earth is transformed, and when mountains are moved into the heart of the seas. (Psalms xlvi. 2, 3.)

16. For I, the Lord thy God, lay hold of thy right hand; (I am he) who saith unto thee: Fear not I will help thee. (Isaiah xli. 13.)

17. Behold, God is my salvation: I will trust and not be afraid; for my strength and song is Yah the Eternal; and he is become my salvation. (Isaiah xii. 2.)

18. O Lord of hosts! happy is the man that trusteth in thee. (Psalms lxxxiv. 13.)

19. Unless the Lord build the house, in vain labor they that build on it; unless the Lord guard the city, in vain is the watchman wakeful. It is in vain for you to be early in rising, to be late in sitting up, eating the bread of painful toils; (for) so doth he give unto his beloved sleep. (Psalms cxxvii. 1, 2.)

20. Trust in the Lord with all thy heart; and upon thine own understanding do not rely. (Proverbs iii. 5.)

21. Trust in the Lord and do good; dwell in the land and feed (thyself with) truthfulness. And delight thyself in the Lord, and he will give thee the wishes of thy heart. Commit thy way unto the Lord, and trust in him: and he will accomplish it. And he will bring forth as the light thy righteousness, and the justice of thy (cause) as the noonday. Be silent before the Lord, and wait patiently for him: fret not thyself because of him who prospereth in his way, because of the man who practices wicked devices. (Psalms xxxvii. 3–7.)

22. Yea, in God hope in silence, my soul, for from him is my expectation. Only he is my rock and my salvation; (he is) my defense; I shall not be moved. With God are my salvation and my glory; the rock of my strength (and) my protection are in God. Trust in him at all times, O ye people; pour out before him your heart: God is our protection for us. Selah. Verily, nought are the sons of (common) men, a lie the sons of (the great) men; they must rise in the balance, they are altogether (lighter) than nought. Do not put your trust in defrauding: and be not rendered vain through robbery: if riches flourish, set not your heart (upon them). Once hath God spoken (yea) twice (what) I have heard; that strength belongeth unto God. (Psalms lxii. 6–12.)

23. "Lo, this is the man that made not God his fortress, but trusted in the abundance of his riches, relied proudly on his mischievous wickedness." But I am like a green olive tree in the house of God; I trust in the kindness of God forever and ever. I will thank thee

forever because thou hast done it; and I will wait on thy name for (it is) good before thy pious ones. (Psalms lii. 9-11.)

24. Thus hath said the Lord, Cursed is the man that trusteth in man and placeth on flesh his dependence, while from the Lord his heart departeth. And he shall be like a lonely tree in the desert, which feeleth not when the good cometh; but abideth in the parched places in the wilderness, in a salty land which can not be inhabited. Blessed is the man that trusteth in the Lord, and the Lord will be his trust. And he shall be like a tree that is planted by the waters, and by a stream spreadeth out its roots, which feeleth not when the heat cometh, but its leaf remaineth green, and in a year of drought it is undisturbed by care and ceaseth not from yielding fruit. (Jeremiah xvii. 5-8.)

25. The Lord is for me, among those that help me; therefore shall I indeed look on (the punishment of) those that hate me. It is better to seek shelter with the Lord than to trust in man. It is better to seek shelter with the Lord than to trust in princes. (Psalms cxviii. 7-9.)

26. Put not your trust in princes, in the son of man in whom there is no salvation. When his spirit goeth forth he returneth to his (native) earth: on that very day perish his thoughts. But happy is he who hath the God of Jacob for his help, whose hope is on the Lord his God, who hath made heaven and earth, the sea and all that is therein; who keepeth truth forever; who doeth justice for the oppressed; who giveth bread to the hungry; the Lord looseneth the prisoners; the Lord causeth the blind to see; the Lord raiseth up those who are bowed down; the Lord loveth the righteous; the Lord guardeth the strangers; the fatherless and widow he helpeth up. (Psalms cxlvi. 3-9.)

27. Cast thy burden upon the Lord, and he will sustain thee; he will never suffer the righteous to be moved. (Psalms lv. 23.)

28. O fear the Lord, ye, his saints; for there is no want to those who fear him. (Psalms xxxiv. 10.)

29. In the fear of the Lord is the strong confidence (of man) and unto his children will it be a place of shelter. (Proverbs xiv. 26.)

30. I have been young, and I am also grown old, yet have I never seen the righteous forsaken nor his seed seeking for bread. (Psalms xxxvii. 25.)

31. But now thus hath said the Lord that created thee, O Jacob, and he that formed thee, O Israel, Fear not, for I have redeemed thee, I have called thee by thy name; mine art thou. Whenever thou passeth through the waters, I am with thee; and through the rivers—they shall not overflow thee; whenever thou walkest through the fire, thou shalt not be scorched; neither shall the flame burn on thee. (Isaiah xliii. 1–2.)

32. I lift up mine eyes unto the mountains; whence shall come my help? My help is from the Lord, the maker of heaven and earth. He will not suffer thy foot to slip; thy keeper doth not slumber. Behold he slumbereth not, and he sleepeth not—the keeper of Israel. The Lord is thy keeper: the Lord is thy shade, he is on thy right hand. By day the sun shall not strike thee, nor the moon by night. The Lord will guard thee against all evil; he will guard thy soul. The Lord will guard thy going out and thy coming in from this time forth and for evermore. (Psalms cxxi.)

33. What? Should we accept the good alone from God, and the evil we should not accept? (Job ii. 10.)

34. The correction of the Lord, my son, do not despise; and feel no loathing for his admonition; because whomever the Lord loveth he admonisheth; and as a father who delighteth in (his) son. (Proverbs iii. 11, 12.)

35. And thou shalt consider in thy heart that as a man chasteneth his son, so doth the Lord thy God chasten thee. (Deuteronomy viii. 5.)

36. Happy is the man whom thou admonishest, O Lord! and teachest him out of thy law. (Psalms xciv. 12.)

37. Behold, happy is the man whom God admonisheth; despise then not the correction of the Almighty. For he it is that woundeth,

and bindeth up; he smiteth, and his hands do heal. In six distresses will he deliver thee; and in seven there shall be no evil touch thee. In famine he redeemeth thee from death; and in war from the power of the sword. Against the scourge of the tongue shalt thou be hidden; and thou needest not be afraid of destruction when it cometh. At destruction and famine canst thou laugh; and thou needest not have any fear of the beasts of the earth. (Job v. 17–22.)

38. The Lord is good, a stronghold on the day of distress; and he knoweth those that trust in him. (Nahum i. 7.)

39. Behold, the eye of the Lord is upon those that fear him, and upon those that hope for his kindness, to deliver from death their soul, and to keep them alive from famine. Our soul waiteth for the Lord: our help and our shield is he. For in him shall our heart rejoice: because in his holy name have we trusted. Let thy kindness O Lord, be upon us, even as we hope in thee. (Psalms xxxiii. 18–22.)

40. Blessed be the Lord; day by day he loadeth us (with benefits); our Lord is our salvation. Selah. Our God is to us the God of salvation; and by the Eternal the Lord are the escapes from death. (Psalms lxviii. 20, 21.)

41. Why art thou cast down, O my soul? and why art thou disquieted within me? Hope thou in God; for I shall yet thank him, the salvation of my countenance and my God. (Psalms xlii. 12.)

VI.—BELIEVE IN GOD AND IN NO SUPERSTITION.

A strong and healthy mind will never allow itself to be troubled by the superstitious beliefs, the ghostly fears and the foolish practices of so many weak-minded people. We should trust firmly in God, knowing that he is wise and just. And, therefore, it is wrong for us to encourage all such lying persons who practice deceit in order to make us believe that they can tell what is going to happen, for this God has wisely hidden from the eyes of all men.

"God can change the lowest to the highest,
Abase the proud, and raise the humble."—*Horace.*

"Is there any other seat of the Divinity than the earth, sea, air, the heavens, and virtuous minds? Why do you seek God elsewhere? He is whatever you see, he is wherever you move."—*Lucan.*

"Nothing is more deceitful in appearance than false religion."—*Livy.*

Prove that the above are true by the following or other stories in the Bible: Examples: II. Chronicles vi.; II. Chronicles xxxii.; Daniel iii, v., vi.

---

1. Ye shall not tempt the Lord your God as ye tempted him in Massah. (Deuteronomy vi. 16.)

2. Harden not your heart as at Meribah, as on the day of the temptation in the wilderness, when your fathers tempted me, proved me, although they had seen my doing. (Psalms xcv. 8, 9.)

3. Yea, they spoke against God: they said, "Will God be able to set in order a table in the wilderness? Behold, he smote the rock, so that waters gushed out, and streams overflowed; shall he also be able to give bread? or can he provide flesh for his people? Because they had not believed in God, and had not trusted in his salvation." (Psalms lxxviii. 19, 20, 22.)

4. Yea, they once more tempted God, and set limits to the Holy One of Israel. They remembered not his hand, the day when he ransomed them from the adversary. (Psalms lxxviii. 41, 42.)

5. But Achaz said, "I will not ask, and I will not tempt the Lord." (Isaiah vii. 12.)

6. There shall not be found among thee any one who causeth hi son or his daughter to pass through the fire, one who useth the divination, one who is an observer of times, or an enchanter, or a conjurer, or a charmer or a consulter with familiar spirits, or a wizard, who inquireth of the dead. For an abomination unto the Lord are all that do these things. (Deuteronomy xviii. 10 12.)

7. And the person that turneth unto such as have familiar spirits,

and unto wizards, to go astray after them—then will I set my face against that person and will cut him off from among his people. (Leviticus xx. 6.)

8. Thus hath said the Lord, Do not habituate yourselves to the way of the nations, and at the signs of the heaven be ye not dismayed; although the nations should be dismayed at them. (Jeremiah x. 2.)

9. I hate those that depend on lying vanities; but I trust indeed in the Lord. (Psalms xxxi. 7.)

10. Happy is the man that maketh the Lord his trust, and turneth not unto the proud nor such as stray aside unto lies. (Psalms xl. 5.)

VII.—WORSHIP GOD WITH AN UPRIGHT HEART.

The feeling to pray, to pour forth our thanks to God for all his loving kindness is deep-seated within every good and moral man. As long as there is a pure, filial relationship between man and God so long will prayer be a necessity. It is natural for a man to commune with God, when he is in harmony with himself and his Maker. There are various ways of praying, but when sincerely performed, the result is ever the same, pleasing to God and exercising a beneficial, moral and educating influence on the one who prays.

> "Prayer is the soul's sincere desire,
> Uttered or unexpressed;
> The motion of a hidden fire,
> That trembles in the breast.

> "Prayer is the burden of a sigh,
> The falling of a tear;
> The upward glancing of an eye,
> When none but God is near.

> "Prayer is the simplest form of speech
> That infant lips can try;
> Prayer the sublimest strains that reach
> The majesty on high."—*James Montgomery.*

"He prayeth best, who loveth best
All things, both great and small."—*Coleridge.*

"No man can pray heartily without learning something."—*Emerson.*

"The first petition that we are to make to Almighty God is for a good conscience, the next for health of mind, and then of body."—*Seneca.*

"Be not afraid to pray—to pray is right."—*Hartly Coleridge.*

"What greater calamity can fall upon a nation than the loss of worship?"—*Emerson.*

"Things sacred should not only not be touched with the hands, but not violated in thought."—*Cicero.*

Prove that the above are true by the following or other stories in the Bible: Example: II. Chronicles xxix.

1. Watch thy foot when thou goest to the house of God. (Ecclesiates iv. 17.)
2. How fearful is this place! this is none other but the house of God, and this is the gate of heaven. (Genesis xxviii. 17.)
3. The Lord is nigh unto those that are broken-hearted, he saveth those that are of a contrite spirit. (Psalms xxxiv. 19.)
4. The Lord is nigh unto all those who call on him, to all who call on him in truth. The desire of those who fear him will he fulfill, and their cry will he hear and save them. (Psalms cxlv. 18, 19.)
5. O Lord! open thou my lips, and my mouth shall declare thy praise. For thou desirest not sacrifice; else would I give it; in burnt offering hast thou no delight. The sacrifices of God are a broken spirit; a broken and a contrite heart, O God, wilt thou not despise. (Psalms li. 17–19.)
6. To my words give ear, O Lord! have regard to my meditation. Listen unto the voice of my loud cry, my King and my God, when unto thee I pray. O Lord, in the morning do thou hear my voice: in the morning will I set in order (my prayer) before thee, and look up with hope. (Psalms v. 2–4.)

OUR RELIGIOUS DUTIES.

7. I, however, will call on God; and the Lord will save me. At evening and morning and noon will I make my complaint and moan; and he heareth my voice. (Psalms lv. 17, 18.)

8. But thou, O Lord, art a shield around me, my glory and he that lifteth up my head. With my voice I call unto the Lord, and he answereth me out of his holy mountain. Selah. I laid myself down and slept: I awoke; for the Lord sustaineth me. (Psalms iii. 4–6.)

9 May the words of my mouth, and the meditation of my heart be acceptable before thee, O Lord, my Rock and my Redeemer. (Psalms xix. 15.)

10. It is lovely to me that the Lord heareth my voice; my supplications, for he hath inclined his ear unto me: therefore throughout all my days will I call on him. The bands of death had compassed me, and the pangs of the nether world had overtaken me; I had met with distress and sorrow. I then called on the name of the Lord, I beseech thee, O Lord! release my soul. Gracious is the Lord and righteous; and our God is merciful. The Lord preserveth the simple; I was in misery and he helped me. Return, O my soul! unto thy rest: for the Lord hath dealt bountifully with thee. For thou hast delivered my soul from death, mine eyes from tears, my feet from falling. (Psalms cxvi. 1–8.)

11. The sacrifice of the wicked is an abomination of the Lord; but the prayer of the upright obtaineth his favor. (Proverbs xv. 8.)

12. And the Lord said, Forasmuch as this people draw near with their mouth, and with their lips do honor me, but have removed their heart far from me, and their fear toward me is but the acquired precept of men: Therefore, behold, I will do yet farther a marvelous work with this people, doing wonder on wonder; so that the wisdom of their wise men shall be lost, and the understanding of their prudent men shall be hidden. (Isaiah xxix. 13, 14.)

13. Because thy kindness is better than life, my lips shall praise thee. Thus will I bless thee while I live; in thy name will I lift up my hands. When I remember thee upon my couch, I meditate on thee in the night-watches. Because thou hast been a help

unto me; and in the shadow of thy wings will I sing rejoicingly. My soul cleaveth unto following thee: me thy right hand upholdeth. (Psalms lxiii. 4, 5, 7-9.)

14. But as for me, in the abundance of thy kindness will I enter thy house; I will bow myself down before thy holy temple in fear of thee. (Psalms v. 8.)

15. Hallelujah: for it is good to sing praises unto our God; for it is comely; (him) becometh praise. (Psalms cxlvii. 1.)

16. I will bless the Lord at all times: continually shall his praise be in my mouth. My soul shall make her boast in the Lord: the humble shall hear it and be rejoiced. O magnify the Lord with me, and let us exalt his name together. I sought the Lord, and he answered me, and from all that I dreaded did he deliver me. This poor man cried, and the Lord heard him, and out of all his distresses did he save him. The angel of the Lord encampeth round about those that fear him, and delivereth them. (Psalms xxiv. 2-8.)

17. Look unto the heavens, and see, and gaze on the skies which are higher than thou. If thou sin, what dost thou effect against him? and if thy transgressions be multiplied, what canst thou do unto him? If thou be righteous, what givest thou him? or what doth he accept out of thy hand? (Job xxxv. 5-7.)

18. Yet turn not aside from following the Lord, and serve ye the Lord with all thy heart. (I. Samuel xii. 20.)

19. When one turneth away his ear so as not to listen to the law, even his prayer becometh an abomination. (Proverbs xxviii. 9.)

20. For the commandment is a lamp, and the law is light; and the way of life are the admonitions of correction. (Proverbs vi. 23.)

21. Offer sacrifices of righteousness and put your trust in the Lord. (Psalms iv. 6.)

22. And Samuel said, "Hath the Lord as much delight in burnt-offerings and in sacrifices as in obeying the voice of the Lord? Behold, to obey is better than sacrifice, and to attend more than the fat of the rams." (I. Samuel xv. 22.)

23. Sacrifice and meat-offering thou desirest not—ears hast thou

hollowed out unto me—burnt-offering and sin-offering thou demandest not. (Psalms xl. 7.)

24. To exercise righteousness and justice is more acceptable to the Lord than sacrifice. (Proverbs xxi. 3.)

25. Hear, O my people, and I will speak; O Israel, and I will testify against thee: God, thy Lord, am I. Not because of thy sacrifices will I reprove thee; and thy burnt-offerings are continually before me. I will not take a bullock out of thy house, nor he-goats out of thy folds. For mine are all the beasts of the forest, the cattle upon a thousand mountains. I know all the fowls of the mountains; whatever moveth on the fields is with me. If I were hungry I would not say it to thee: for mine is the world and what filleth it. Do I eat the flesh of fatted bulls or drink the blood of he-goats? Offer unto God thanksgiving, and pay unto the Most High thy vows; and call on me on the day of distress, I will deliver thee; and so wilt thou glorify me. (Psalms l. 7-15.)

26. And Solomon now placed himself before the altar of the Lord in the presence of all the congregation of Israel, and spread forth his hands toward Heaven; and he said, O Lord, the God of Israel, there is no God like thee in the heavens above or on the earth beneath, thou who keepest the convenant and the kindness for thy servants that walk before thee with all their heart. For in truth will God then dwell on the earth? Behold, the heavens and the heavens of heavens can not contain thee: how much less then this house which I have built! Yet wilt thou turn unto the prayer of thy servant and to his supplication, O Lord, my God, to listen unto the entreaty and unto the prayer which thy servant prayeth before thee to-day; that thine eyes may be open toward this house night and day, toward the place of which thou hast said, My name shall be there; that thou mayest listen unto the prayer which thy servant shall pray at this place: And listen thou to the supplication of thy servant and thy people, Israel, which they will pray at this place: O do thou hear in heaven, thy dwelling-place; and hear and forgive. What prayer and supplication soever be made by any man of all thy people Israel, when they shall be conscious,

every man of the plague of his own heart, and he then spread forth his hands toward this house. Then do thou hear in heaven, the place of thy dwelling, and forgive, and act, and give to every man in accordance with all his ways, as thou mayest know his heart; for thou thyself alone knowest the heart of all the children of men; in order that they may fear thee all the days that they live on the face of the land which thou hast given unto our fathers. But also to the stranger who is not of thy people Israel, but cometh out of a far-off country for the sake of thy name; for they will hear of thy great name, and of thy strong hand, and of thy outstretched arm; when he will come and pray at this house: Mayest thou listen in heaven, the place of thy dwelling, and do according to all that the stranger will call on thee for; in order that all the nations of the earth may know thy name, to fear thee as (do) thy people Israel: and that they may understand that this house which I have built is called by thy name. (I. Kings viii. 22, 23, 27–30, 38–43.)

27. O come, let us sing unto the Lord: let us shout joyfully to the rock of our salvation. Let us come before his presence with thanksgiving, and shout joyfully unto him with psalms. For a great God is the Lord, and a great King above all Gods; in whose hand are the deep places of the earth; and whose are the heights of the mountains; whose is the sea and who hath made it; and whose hands have formed the dry land, O come and let us prostrate ourselves and bow down : let us kneel before the Lord our Maker. For he is our God, and we are the people of his pasture and the flock of his hand: Yea, this day if ye will hearken unto his voice. (Psalms xcv. 1–7.)

28. Take with you words and return to the Lord; say unto him, "Pardon all (our) iniquity and accept (our return to) good : and let us repay the steers (of sacrifice) with (the prayer of) our lips." (Hosea xiv. 3.)

29. In assemblies bless ye God (praise) the Lord, ye sprung from Israel's fountain. (Psalms lxviii. 27.)

VIII.—LET THE OBSERVANCE OF THE SABBATHS AND HOLIDAYS AND YOUR ATTENDANCE AT THE PLACE AND PARTAKING IN ALL MATTERS OF WORSHIP BE A FIXED AND EARNEST DUTY ALL THROUGH LIFE.

The great blessings which God has given us in our Sabbaths and holidays must ever be remembered, and their observance will ever be a joy and benefit to us. Men may so fix their attention and their affections on the pleasures and pursuits of the world as to forget every higher and nobler purpose, to forget that at any moment death may come, and all the work, worry and unrest with which we burden ourselves will prove to be vain. To teach this and to prevent our losing ourselves in worldliness our Sabbaths and holidays are given to us. By ceasing from our labors and observing them, especially if it be at some cost and sacrifice, we prove thereby that we are free, that we regard the claims of our spiritual natures over our merely bodily wants, and that the cultivation of our religious and moral nature is the truest and best, as it is the highest aim of life. Each one of these sacred days has many special lessons to teach, which, if we mind them, will surely better us—but in general they all give us a time for reflection and devotion, make us forget our cares and give us new trust and strength to bear them by our communion with God.

They give us rest in mind and body, and afford the laboring animals also that rest which all creatures must have, and which makes them able to do better work then and after, which gives them that vitality which lengthens life. But most of all these Sabbaths and holidays are of untold good in that they afford the time and the means for bringing families together, for binding firmer the domestic ties of love which are the one great source of pure and useful and happy lives.

> "O day of rest! how beautiful, how fair,
> How welcome to the weary and the old!
> Day of the Lord, and truce to earthly care,
> Day of the Lord, as all our days should be."—*Longfellow.*

> "Take rest, a field that has rested gives a bountiful crop."—*Ovid.*

> "Straining breaks the bow, and relaxation relieves the mind."—*Syrus.*

Prove the truth of the above by the following or other stories of the Bible: Examples: II. Samuel vi.; II. Chronicles vii.; Nehemiah viii.; II. Chronicles xxxv.

---

1. And the Lord spoke unto Moses, saying, Speak unto the children of Israel and say unto them, The feasts of the Lord, which ye shall proclaim to be holy convocation—these are my feasts. Six days may work be done; but on the seventh day is the Sabbath of rest, a holy convocation, no kind of work shall ye do thereon, it is the Sabbath (holy) unto the Lord in all your dwellings. (Leviticus xxiii. 1–3.)

2. And the children of Israel shall keep the Sabbath, to observe the Sabbath throughout their generations, for a perpetual covenant. Between me and the children of Israel it shall be a sign forever; for in six days the Lord made the heavens and the earth, and on the seventh day he rested, and was refreshed. (Exodus xxxi. 16, 17.)

3. Remember the Sabbath day to keep it holy. Six days shalt thou labor and do all thy work. But the seventh day is the Sabbath in honor of the Lord thy God: on it thou shalt not do any work, neither thou, nor thy son, nor thy daughter, thy man-servant, nor thy maid servant, nor thy cattle, nor thy stranger that is within thy gates. For in six days the Lord made the heavens and the earth, the sea, and all that is in them, and rested on the seventh day; therefore the Lord blessed the seventh day and hallowed it. (Exodus xx. 8–11.)

4. On the fourteenth day of the first month* toward evening is the Passover-lamb to be offered unto the Lord. And on the fifteenth day of the same month is the feast of unleavened bread unto the Lord; seven days must ye eat unleavened bread. (Leviticus xxiii. 5, 6.)

5. And on the first day there shall be a holy convocation, and on the seventh day there shall be a holy convocation to you; no manner of work shall be done on them, save what is eaten by every man, that only may be prepared by you. And ye shall observe the unleavened bread; for on this self-same day have I brought your armies out of the land of Egypt; therefore shall ye observe this day in your generations as an ordinance forever. (Exodus xii. 16, 17.)

6. Seven weeks shalt thou number unto thyself: from the time thou beginnest to put the sickle to the corn, shalt thou begin to number seven weeks. And thou shalt keep the feast of weeks unto the Lord thy God with a tribute of a free will offering of thy hand, which thou shalt give, according as the Lord thy God shall have blessed thee. And thou shalt rejoice before the Lord thy God, thou, and thy son, and thy daughter, and thy man-servant, and thy maid-servant, and the Levite that is within thy gates, and the stranger, and the fatherless, and the widow that are in the midst of thee, in the place which the Lord thy God will choose to let his name dwell there, and thou shalt remember that thou hast been a bondman in Egypt; and thou shalt observe and do these statutes. (Deuteronomy xvi. 9–12.)

7. And in the seventh month, on the first day of the month, shall ye have a holy convocation; no servile work shall ye do; a day of blowing of the cornet shall it be unto you. (Numbers xxix. 1.)

8. And it shall be unto you a statute forever: in the seventh month, on the tenth of the month, shall ye afflict yourselves, and no work shall ye do, whether it be one of your own country or the stranger that sojourneth among you. For on that day shall (the

---

* The names of the months according to the Hebrew calendar are: Nissan, Iyar, Sivan, Tamuz, Ab, Ellul, Tishri, Heshvan, Kislev, Tebeth, Shebat, Adar, and in leap-year Adar Sheni or Second Adar.

high-priest) make an atonement for you to cleanse you: from all your sins before the Lord shall ye be clean. (Leviticus xvi. 29, 30.)

9. No manner of work shall ye do; it shall be a statute forever throughout your generations, in all your dwellings a Sabbath of rest it shall be unto you, and ye shall afflict yourselves: on the ninth day of the month at evening (shall ye begin), from evening unto evening shall ye celebrate your Sabbath. (Leviticus xxiii. 31, 32.)

10. The feast of tabernacles shalt thou hold for thyself seven days, when thou hast gathered in the produce of thy threshing floor and of thy wine-press. And thou shalt rejoice on thy feast, thou, and thy son, and thy daughter, and thy man-servant, and thy maid-servant and the Levite, and the stranger, and the fatherless and the widow that are within thy gates. Seven days shalt thou keep a solemn feast unto the Lord thy God in the place which the Lord will choose; because the Lord thy God will bless thee in all thy product, and in all the work of thy hands, and thou shalt only rejoice. (Deuteronomy xvi. 13-15.)

11. But on the fifteenth day of the seventh month, when ye have gathered in the fruit of the land, shall ye keep the feast of the Lord seven days; on the first day shall be a rest, and on the eighth day shall be a rest. And ye shall take unto yourselves on the first day the fruit of the tree hadar, branches of palm trees and the boughs of the myrtle tree, and willows of the brook; and ye shall rejoice before the Lord thy God seven days. And ye shall keep it as a feast unto the Lord seven days in the year: it shall be a statute forever throughout your generations; in the seventh month shall ye celebrate it. In booths shall ye dwell seven days; all that are Israelites born shall dwell in booths. In order that your generations may know, that I caused the children of Israel to dwell in booths, when I brought them forth out of the land of Egypt: I am the Lord thy God. And Moses declared the feasts of the Lord unto the children of Israel. (Leviticus xxiii. 39-44.)

12. And they beautified the exterior of the temple with golden crowns and with shields, and they built the gate, and they put up the

doors. And all the people rejoiced exceedingly, for God had ended their shame in the midst of the people. And Jehudah and his brothers and all the house of Israel took upon themselves to celebrate (Chanuka) the days of the dedication of the temple with rejoicing and thanksgiving in its due seasons, for eight days from the fifteenth day of the month of Kislev, from year to year. (Maccabee iv.)

13. The Jews confirmed it as a duty, and took upon themselves, and upon their seed, and upon all such as join themselves unto them, so that no one should fail therein that they would celebrate these two days according to their prescription and at their appointed time in each and every year. And these days are remembered and celebrated throughout each and every generation, every family, every province and every city; and these days of Purim will not pass away from the midst of the Jews, nor will their memorial cease from their seed. To confirm these days of Purim in their times, just as Mordecai the Jew and Esther the Queen had enjoined on them, and as they had confirmed for themselves and for their seed the matters of the fasting and their prayers. (Esther ix. 27, 28, 31.)

14. Therefore do the Jews make the fourteenth day of the month of Adar as one of joy and entertainment and a feast-day and of sending gifts one to another. (Esther ix. 9.)

E.—MAN AND HIS MISSION.

I.—MAN IS THE NOBLEST OF GOD'S WORKS.

Great are the wonders with which God has surrounded us, everywhere they unroll themselves before us in awe-inspiring splendor. There is no mineral, no plant, no fish in the water, no animal on earth, no bird nor insect in the air, in which God's power, wisdom and loving kindness are not displayed. But the greatest wonder of all creation is man. With us and in us creation has reached its loftiest point. Man through his reason, which raises him above the lower animals, through his faculty to distinguish the right from the wrong, and through his power to realize the lofty mission for which all these great gifts have been bestowed upon him, has become godlike.

"Let each man think himself an art of God,
His mind a thought, his life a breath of God."—*Baily.*

"An honest man is the noblest work of God."—*Pope.*

"What a piece of work is man, how noble in reason! how infinite in faculty! in form and moving how admirable! in action how like an angel! in apprehension how like a God!"—*Shakespeare.*

"Every one is in a small way the image of God."—*Lucretius.*

1. And God said, Let us make man in our image, after our likeness; and they shall have dominion over the fish of the sea, and over the fowl of the heaven, and over the cattle, and over all the earth, and over every creeping thing that creepeth upon the earth. And God created man in his image, in the image of God created he him: male and female created he them. And God blessed them, and God said unto them, Be fruitful and multiply, fill the earth and

subdue it; and have dominion over the fish of the sea and over the fowl of the heaven, and over every living thing that moveth upon the earth. (Genesis i. 26–28.)

2. Blessed are ye of the Lord, who made heaven and earth. The heavens are the heavens of the Lord; but the earth has he given to the children of men. (Psalms cxv. 15, 16.)

3. When I behold thy heavens, the work of thy fingers, the moon and the stars which thou hast established:—What is mortal, that thou rememberest him? and the son of man that thou thinkest of him? Yet thou hast made him but a little less than angels, and hast crowned him with honor and glory. Thou hast given him dominion over the works of thy hands; everything hast thou placed beneath his feet; flocks and herds altogether, and also the beasts of the field; the birds of heaven and the fishes of the sea, whatsoever passeth through the paths of the sea. O Eternal One our Lord! how excellent is thy name on all the earth. (Psalms viii. 4–10.)

4. Lord, what is man, that thou takest cognizance of him! the son of a mortal that thou regardest him! (Psalms cxliv. 3.)

5. Lo! this only did I find, that God hath made man upright. (Ecclesiastes vii. 29.)

6. All my bones will say, "Lord! who is like unto thee?" (Psalms xxxv. 10.)

7. I will thank thee, therefore, that I am (so) fearfully (and) wonderfully made: wonderful are thy works; and that my soul knoweth right well. (Psalms cxxxix. 14.)

8. And the Lord God formed man of dust from the ground, and breathed into his nostrils the breath of life, and the man became a living being. (Genesis ii. 7.)

9. The spirit of God hath made me, and the breath of the Almighty giveth me life. (Job xxxiii. 4.)

10. The Lord who stretcheth forth the heavens, and layeth the foundation of the earth, and formeth the spirit of man within him. (Zechariah xii. 1.)

11. And thy good spirit thou gavest to make him intelligent. (Nehemiah ix. 20.)

12. Who hath given a mouth to man? or who maketh him dumb or deaf, or seeing or blind? is it not I the Lord? (Exodus iv. 11.)

13. The spirit of the Lord spoke through me and his word was upon my tongue. (II. Samuel xxiii. 2.)

II.—MAN HAS FREE WILL AND CONSCIENCE.

By giving a man freedom and liberty to act according to the best of his knowledge, we show him thereby a special distinction and favor.

However, we can only safely grant such permission to the best and most learned. In this we merely follow the loving example which our Heavenly Father has set us. The highest and best with which he has crowned creation is man, and to show his loving kindness for man, he has given him a *free will* and the knowledge how to act that we may find favor in the eyes of man and before our God. This sublime gift would have been sufficient to thank our Father night and day, but God gave us still more. That by which we know whether we do not abuse this great gift, and this the greatest of all benefits with which God has blest us is "Conscience." It is the still small voice within us that is ever awake, is ever a witness to all our deeds. It applauds us when our deeds are good, true and beautiful, but it rebukes in a loud and terrible voice when we do what is displeasing to God and man.

"A good conscience is to the soul what health is to the body; it preserves a constant ease and serenity within us, and more than countervails all the calamities and afflictions which can possibly befall us."—*Addison*.

"Thou mayest conceal thy sin by cunning art,
But conscience sits a witness in the heart,
Which will disturb thy peace, thy rest undo,
For that is witness, judge and prison, too."

1. And the Lord God said, Behold, the man is become as one of us, to know good and evil. (Genesis iii. 22.)
2. See, I have set before thee this day life and the good, death and the evil. (Deuteronomy xxx. 15.)
3. I call heaven and earth as witnesses against you this day that I have set before you life and death, the blessing and the curse: therefore choose thou life in order that thou mayest live, both thou and thy seed. (Deuteronomy xxx. 19.)
4. If thou dost well shalt thou not be accepted? and if thou dost not well, sin lieth at the door; and unto thee is its desire, but thou canst rule over it. (Genesis iv. 7.)
5. Seek for the good, and not the evil, in order that ye may live; and so will the Lord, the God of hosts, be with you, as ye have said. Hate the evil, and love the good, and establish justice firmly in the gate. (Amos v. 14, 15.)
6. One that is slow to anger is better than a hero, and he that ruleth his spirit, than the conqueror of a city. (Proverbs xvi. 32.)
7. Like a city that is broken in and is without walls, so is the man that hath no control over his spirit. (Proverbs xxv. 28.)
8. Woe unto those that say of the evil it is good, and of the good it is evil; that put darkness for light, and light for darkness; that put bitter for sweet and sweet for bitter! (Isaiah v. 20.)
9. Be ye not like the horse, or like the mule, who hath no understanding, who must be held in with bit and bridle, his ornament, lest he come near unto thee. (Psalms xxxii. 9.)
10. Man, though in splendor, who understandeth not, is like the beasts that perish. (Psalms xlix. 21.)
11. Happy is the man that always dreadeth (to do evil); but he that hardeneth his heart will fall into unhappiness. (Proverbs xxviii. 14.)
12. The way of the wicked is like darkness; they know not against whom they stumble. (Proverbs iv. 19.)
13. O that thou hadst but listened to my commandments! then

would have been as a river thy peace and thy prosperity as the waves of the sea. (Isaiah xlviii. 18.)

14. Light is sown for the righteous, and joy for the upright in heart. (Psalms xcvii. 11.)

15. Say ye to the righteous that he hath done well: for the fruit of their doings shall they eat. Woe unto the wicked that doeth evil: for the recompense of his hands shall be bestowed on him. (Isaiah iii. 10, 11.)

16. The righteousness of the perfect maketh even his way; but by his own wickedness will the wicked fall. (Proverbs xi. 5.)

17. He that walketh uprightly, ever walketh securely: but he that perverteth his ways will be punished. (Proverbs x. 9.)

18. Perverse is the way of the man that is estranged (from goodness); but as for the pure his work is upright. (Proverbs. xxi. 8.)

19. If I be wicked, woe unto me. (Job x. 15.)

20. But the wicked are like the troubled sea: for it can never be at rest, but the waters cast up mire and dirt. There is no peace, saith my God, to the wicked. (Isaiah lvii. 20, 21.)

21. There is no peace, saith the Lord, unto the wicked. (Isaiah xlviii. 22.)

22. In my heart have I treasured up thy saying, in order that I may not sin against thee. (Psalms cxix. 11.)

23. In everlasting remembrance shall the righteous be held. Of an evil report shall he not be afraid; his heart is firm, trusting in the Lord. (Psalms cxii. 6, 7.)

24. Abundant peace have they who love thy law: and there is nothing that causeth them to stumble. (Psalms cxix. 165.)

III.—THE SOUL OF MAN IS IMMORTAL.

Men live the number of years allotted to them and then they die. But this is not the end. Our souls live on. This truth God has revealed to us by his voice within us, by the works of nature about us,

MAN AND HIS MISSION.

by the higher hopes and aspirations which he has implanted in our hearts and to realize which fully this life is too short.

> "Oh! the souls of those that die
> Are but sunbeams lifted higher." —*Longfellow.*

> "What'er of earth is formed to earth returns,
> The soul of man alone, that particle divine,
> Escapes the wreck of worlds when all things fail!"
> —*Somerville.*

"God being all-wise would not destroy the intellect he created, being all-good he would not disappoint the highest hope with which he impresses us; and being all-just he could not have commanded man only to subordinate his carnal inclinations to his spiritual welfare, if the soul were not destined to everlasting life."—*I. M. Wise.*

1. When the dust will return to the earth as it was, and the spirit will return unto God who gave it. (Ecclesiates xii. 7.)

2. Yet will the soul of my Lord be bound in the bond of life with the Lord thy God. (I. Samuel xxv. 29.)

3. But God will redeem my soul from the power of the nether world; for he will take me away. Selah. (Psalms xlix. 16.)

4. Therefore is rejoiced my heart, and my spirit is glad: also my flesh shall rest in safety. For thou wilt not abandon my soul to the grave: thou wilt not suffer thy pious (servant) to see corruption. Thou wilt let me know the path of life; fulness of joy is in thy presence: pleasures are at thy right hand for evermore. (Psalms xvi. 9-11.)

5. Return, O my soul, unto thy rest; for the Lord hath dealt bountifully with thee. For thou hast delivered my soul from death, mine eyes from tears, my feet from falling. I will walk before the Lord in the lands of life. (Psalms cxvi. 7-9.)

6. When a wicked man dieth (his) hope vanisheth; and the expectation of (his) children is lost. (Proverbs xi. 7.)

7. For surely there is a future, and thy hope will not be cut off. (Proverbs xxiii. 18.)

IV.—IT IS MAN'S MISSION TO TRY AND PERFECT HIS MORAL, MENTAL AND PHYSICAL NATURES.

By our moral, mental and physical natures, we are distinguished from all other creatures. These qualities when they reach perfection in man make him godlike, lead him to happiness and to the realization of that divine mission for which he has been put on earth. To be gifted with the highest powers in creation and then basely abuse them is degrading, is lowering ourselves to the level of the brutes.

It is our sacred duty, therefore, to labor and strive in all our enterprises to reach the ideal of moral, mental and physical perfection, for our own good as well as for the good of all mankind.

"Every man is bound to consecrate his every faculty to its fulfillment."—*Mazzini.*

"Man was born for two things—*thinking* and *acting.*"—*Cicero.*

"The consciousness of having developed our moral and intellectual capacities according to the will of God, and elevated ourselves to a higher order of spirits, is of itself a gracious reward, when egotism and carnal passions have vanished. And the consciousness of being one of the lower order of spirits by our own errors and sins is a mortifying punishment."—*Isaac M. Wise.*

1. The path of life (leadeth) upward for the intelligent, in order that he may avoid the nether world beneath. (Proverbs xv. 24.)

2. The highway of the upright is to depart from evil; he preserveth his soul that watcheth his way. (Proverbs xvi. 17.)

3. But the path of the righteous is as the early morning light that shineth more and more brightly until the height of noon-day. (Proverbs iv. 18.)

4. On the path of righteousness there is life; and on her pathway there is immortality. (Proverbs xii. 28.)

5. Hear counsel and accept correction, in order that thou mayest be wise in thy latter end. (Proverbs xix. 20.)

6. Happy is the man that hath found wisdom, and the man that acquireth understanding. For the obtaining of her is better than the obtaining of silver, and better than fine gold is her product. She is more precious than pearls; and all the things thou valuest are not equal unto her. Length of days is in her right hand; in her left are riches and honor. Her ways are ways of pleasantness and all her paths are peace. A tree of life is she to those that lay hold on her; and every one that firmly graspeth her will be made happy. (Proverbs iii. 13-18.)

7. Then wilt thou understand righteousness, and justice, and equity; yea, every track of goodness. For wisdom will enter thy heart, and knowledge will be pleasant unto thy soul. (Proverbs ii. 9, 10.)

8 He that reflecteth on a matter wisely will find happiness; and whoso trusteth in the Lord — happiness attend him! (Proverbs xvi. 20.)

9. The desire of the righteous is only good; but the hope of the wicked is the wrath (of God). (Proverbs xi. 23.)

10. He that diligently searcheth after good seeketh favor; but if one inquire after evil, it will come unto him. (Proverbs xi. 27.)

11. Of all perfection have I seen the end; (but) thy commandment is exceedingly extended. O how do I love thy law! all the day is it my meditation. (Psalms cxix. 96, 97.)

12. From every evil path have I withholden my feet, in order that I might observe thy word. From thy ordinance have I not departed; for thou hast instructed me. How much sweeter are to my palate thy sayings than honey to my mouth. Through thy precepts shall I obtain understanding; therefore do I hate every path of falsehood. A lamp unto my feet is thy word and a light unto my path. (Psalms cxix. 101-105.)

V.—IT IS THE DUTY OF EVERY ONE OF US TO SO ACT THAT HIS ACTIONS SHALL SERVE AS A MODEL TO OTHERS.

In all our actions and undertakings one question ought ever be before us, viz : Would I approve this act or undertaking if others were to engage upon it, or do it to me or to those near and dear to me? Much pain, much sorrow, many a sleepless, painful night would not have been endured had we but put this question to ourselves when we were about to do something that was not for our benefit nor for that of our fellow-men. Most moral teaching is done by the example which we have before us. As our parents and superiors act, we are apt to act, and as we act those whom we serve as an example will act. If our example is good our reward is double; we benefit ourselves and a large number of others besides. If our example is bad our guilt is great, for the seeds of corruption which we thus scatter grow and grow till they bring endless pain and grief and unpardonable sin.

1. Now, therefore, if ye will obey my voice indeed and keep my covenant, then ye shall be a peculiar treasure unto me above all people, for all the earth is mine. And ye shall be unto me a kingdom of priests and a holy nation. These are the words which thou shalt speak unto the children of Israel. (Exodus xix. 5, 6.)

2. Ye shall be named the priests of the Lord, men shall call you the ministers of our God. (Isaiah lxi. 6.)

3. Remember these, O Jacob and Israel; for thou art my servants; O Israel, thou shalt not be forgotten of me. (Isaiah xliv. 21.)

4. Behold my servant whom I uphold, mine elect, in whom my soul delighteth, I have put my spirit upon him, he shall bring forth judgment to the Gentiles. (Isaiah xlii. 1.)

5. This people have I formed for myself; they shall show forth my praise. (Isaiah xliii. 21.)

6. In Judah God is known; his name is great in Israel. (Psalms lxxvi. 2.)

7. Speak to all the congregation of the children of Israel, and say unto them: Ye shall be holy, for I, the Lord your God, am holy. (Leviticus xix. 2.)

8. Holy men shall ye be unto me. (Exodus xxii. 30.)

9. Ye shall be holy unto me, for I, the Lord, am holy, and have separated you from other people that ye should be mine. (Leviticus xx. 26.)

10. And they shall call them the holy people, the redeemed of the Lord. (Isaiah xlii. 12.)

11. A holy people art thou unto the Lord thy God, and the Lord hath chosen thee to be a peculiar people unto himself, above all the nations that are upon the earth. (Deuteronomy xiv. 2.)

12. The Lord did not set his love upon you nor choose you because you were more in number than any people, for ye were the fewest of all people. But because the Lord loved you and because he would keep the oath which he had sworn unto your fathers. (Deuteronomy vii. 6–8.)

13. You only have I known of all the families of the earth. (Amos iii. 2.)

14. Keep, therefore, (my statutes) and do them, for this is your wisdom and your understanding in the sight of the nations, which shall hear all these statutes and say: Surely this great nation is a wise and understanding people. And what nation is there so great that have statutes and judgments so righteous as all this law which I set before you this day? (Deuteronomy iv. 6–8.)

15. The knowledge of the holy is understanding. (Proverbs ix. 10.)

VI.—IT IS OUR SACRED DUTY TO PRESERVE AND LIVE UP TO OUR INHERITED FAITH.

Our religion has civilized and enlightened men, and they by their cultivating the divine lessons which it teaches, have acquired knowledge and understanding whereby they have brought into existence all those blessings of civilization which surround us. All this our ancestors have secured for us, not infrequently at great sacrifices. Shall we merely reap the hard-earned benefits of their labors? Shall we remain inactive, do nothing for the cause of religion? Just as soon as we desist from learning and teaching our religion and practicing its sublime lessons, so soon do we fall back into ignorance, into that state of barbarism, a mere description of which fills us with horror. We owe it to those who are to come after us to take proper care of that sacred treasure, our holy religion, which God and our forefathers have bequeathed unto us.

1. Moses commanded us a law, even the inheritance of the congregation of Jacob. (Deuteronomy xxxiii. 4.)

2. He established a testimony in Jacob and appointed a law in Israel, which he commanded our fathers, that they should make them known to their children; that the generation to come might know them, even the children which should be born who should arise and declare them to their children. (Psalms lxxviii. 5, 6.)

3. Neither with you only do I make this covenant and this oath, but with him that standeth here with us this day before the Lord our God, and also with him that is not here with us this day. (Deuteronomy xxix. 13, 14.)

4. Be of good courage and let us be valiant for our people and for the cities of our God, and the Lord do that which is good in his sight (I. Chronicles xix. 13.)

5. The Lord is the portion of mine inheritance and of my cup, thou maintainest my lot. The lines are fallen unto me in pleasant places, yea, I have a goodly heritage. I will bless the Lord, who hath given me counsel. (Psalms xvi. 5–7.)

6. Thus saith the Lord, Let not the wise man glory in his wisdom, neither let the mighty man glory in his might, let not the rich man

glory in his riches; but let him that glorieth glory in this, that he understandeth and knoweth me that I am the Lord which exercise loving kindness, judgment and righteousness in the earth, for in these things I delight, saith the Lord. (Jeremiah ix. 22, 23.)

7. Know thou the God of thy father and serve him with a perfect heart and with a willing mind, for the Lord searcheth all hearts, and understandeth all the imaginations of the thoughts. (I. Chronicles xxviii. 9.)

8. We shall know, if we follow on to know the Lord, his going forth is prepared as the morning, and he shall come unto us as the rain. (Hosea vi. 3.)

9. For I desired mercy and not sacrifice, and the knowledge of God more than burnt-offerings. (Hosea vi. 6)

10. The grass withereth, the flower fadeth, but the word of our God shall stand forever. (Isaiah xl. 8.)

11. The law of the Lord is perfect, converting the soul, the testimony of the Lord is sure, making wise the simple. The statutes of the Lord are right, rejoicing the heart. The commandment of the Lord is pure, enlightening the eyes. The fear of the Lord is clean, enduring forever. The judgments of the Lord are true and righteous altogether. More to be desired are they than gold, yea, than much fine gold, sweeter also than honey and the honey-comb. (Psalms xix. 8–11.)

12. Unless the law had been my delights, I should then have perished in mine affliction. I will never forget thy precepts, for with them thou hast quickened me. (Psalms cxix 92, 93.)

13. The law of thy mouth is better unto me than thousands of gold and silver. (Psalms cxix. 72.)

VII.—IT IS OUR SACRED DUTY TO KEEP FROM SINNING AND TO REPENT OF OUR EVIL DOINGS.

However young, however limited our experiences are, we can not fail to make one observation, namely, sin has never yet brought good.

It almost always leads to deserved punishment, and when the wrong-doer does sometimes escape from being detected, his conscience has given him more pain than any punishment could have done. Why, then, should we continue to sin, when it brings us and others no good but endless evil? Yet man's moral nature is sometimes weak. Often we are led to sin, even against our will. The evil has been done, but much of its pain can be allayed by sincere repentance. By it God and our wronged neighbors become again reconciled to us. Moreover sincere repentance will guard us from committing in the future a similar wrong.

> " Who after his transgression doth repent
> Is half or altogether innocent."—*Herrick.*

> " Angels for the good man's sin
> Weep to record and blush to give in."—*Campbell.*

"I could not live in peace if I put the shadow of a woful sin between myself and God."—*George Eliot.*

" Great sins make great sufferers."—*A. K. Green.*

Prove the truth of the above by the following or other stories in the Bible: Examples: I. Samuel vii.; I. Kings xxi.; Nehemiah ix.; Job xxii.

1. Who can say I have made my heart clean, I am pure from my sin? (Proverbs xx. 9.)
2. For there is not a just man upon earth that doeth good and sinneth not. (Ecclesiastes vii. 20.)
3. There is no rest in my bones because of my sin, for mine iniquities are gone over my head, as a heavy burden they are too heavy for me. (Psalms xxxviii. 4, 5.)
4. My God, I am ashamed and blush to lift up my face to thee, my God, for our iniquities are increased over our heads, and our trespass is grown up unto the heavens. (Ezra ix. 6.)

5. One sinner destroyeth much good. (Ecclesiastes ix. 18.)

6. Evil pursueth sinners, but to the righteous good shall be repaid. (Proverbs xiii. 21.)

7. For the Lord knoweth the way of the righteous, but the way of the ungodly shall perish. (Psalms i. 6.)

8. If thou, Lord, shouldst mark iniquities, O Lord, who shall stand? (Psalms cxxx. 3.)

9. Teach us to number our days, that we may apply our hearts unto wisdom. (Psalms xc. 12.)

10. As I live, saith the Lord God, I have no pleasure in the death of the wicked: but that the wicked turn from his way and live. (Ezekiel xxxiii. 11.)

11. Cast away from you all your transgressions, whereby ye have transgressed, and make yourselves a new heart and a new spirit, for why will ye die, O house of Israel? For I have no pleasure in the death of him that dieth, saith the Lord God, wherefore turn and live ye. (Ezekiel xviii. 31, 32.)

12. Return, thou backsliding Israel, saith the Lord, and I will not cause mine anger to fall upon you, for I am merciful, saith the Lord, and I will not keep anger forever. (Jeremiah iii. 12.)

13. Return ye, backsliding children, and I will heal your backsliding. Behold we come unto thee, for thou art the Lord our God. (Jeremiah iii. 22.)

14. Turn ye to me with all your heart, and with fasting, and with weeping, and with mourning; and rend your heart and not your garment, and turn unto the Lord your God, for he is gracious and merciful, slow to anger, and of great kindness, and repenteth him of the evil. (Joel ii. 12, 13.)

15. He that covereth his sins shall not prosper; but whoso confesseth and forsaketh them shall have mercy. (Proverbs xxviii. 13.)

16. Let the wicked forsake his way, and the unrighteous man his thoughts; and let him return unto the Lord and he will have mercy upon him, and to our God, for he will abundantly pardon. (Isaiah lv. 7)

17. Behold the Lord's hand is not shortened, that it can not save; neither his ear heavy, that it can not hear. But your iniquities have separated between you and your God, and your sins have hid his face from you, that he will not hear. (Isaiah lix. 1, 2.)

VIII. — THE GOOD ARE REWARDED, THE BAD ARE PUNISHED.

The conviction that the good will be rewarded and the bad will be punished is deeply rooted within us. The sense of right and justice which God has implanted in our hearts and minds, and our knowledge of God as a just and a righteous judge, confirm this conviction. Furthermore, along with this conviction goes our firm confidence in the truth of the promise of a future life, which our religion teaches. What this future life is we do not know. Our religion teaches that all good and moral men, no matter what their religion, will share the blessings of the life to come. Judgment comes. Those who have escaped their merited punishment, or have been deprived of their due rewards in this life, must be dealt with in the life that is to come according to their guilt or merits.

"Disbelief in futurity lessens in a great measure the ties of morality, and may be supposed for that reason to be pernicious to civil society."—*Hume*.

Show the truth of the above from the following or other stories of the Bible: Examples: Job v., viii., ix., xv., xxiv.; Isaiah ii.

1. Therefore hearken unto me, ye men of understanding, far be it from God that he should do wickedness; and from the Almighty that he should commit iniquity. For the work of a man shall he render unto him, and cause every man to find according to his ways. Yea, surely God will not do wickedly, neither will the Almighty pervert judgment. (Job xxxiv. 10-12.)

2. For God shall bring every work into judgment, with every

secret thing, whether it be good or whether it be evil. (Ecclesiastes xii. 14.)

3. Rejoice, O young man, in thy youth; and let thy heart cheer thee in the days of thy youth, and walk in the ways of thy heart, and in the sight of thine eyes; but know thou that for all these things God will bring thee unto judgment. (Ecclesiastes xi. 9.)

4. Behold the righteous shall be recompensed on the earth, how much more the wicked and the sinner. (Proverbs xi. 31.)

5. Unto thee, O Lord, belongeth mercy, for thou rendereth to every man according to his work. (Psalms lxii. 13.)

6. The curse of the Lord is in the house of the wicked, but he blesseth the habitation of the just. (Proverbs iii. 33.)

7. Then shall ye return and discern between the righteous and the wicked, between him that serveth God and him that serveth him not. For, behold, the day cometh that shall burn as an oven; and all the proud, yea, and all that do wickedly shall be stubble: and the day that cometh shall burn them up, saith the Lord of hosts, that it shall leave them neither root nor branch. But unto you that fear my name shall the sun of righteousness arise with healing in his wings. (Malachi iii. 18-21.)

8. He that soweth iniquity shall reap vanity, and the rod of his anger shall fade. (Proverbs xxii. 8.)

9. They that sow in tears shall reap in joy. He that goeth forth and weepeth, bearing precious seed, shall doubtless come again with rejoicing, bring in his sheaves with him. (Psalms cxxvi. 5, 6.)

10. The righteous shall flourish like the palm tree, he shall grow like a cedar in Lebanon. Those that be planted in the house of the Lord shall flourish in the courts of our God. To show that the Lord is upright, he is my rock, and there is no unrighteousness in him. (Psalms xcii. 13, 14, 16.)

11. As for me, I will behold thy face in righteousness, I shall be satisfied, when I awake, with thy likeness. (Psalms xvii. 15.)

IX.—IT IS OUR SACRED DUTY TO OBEY AND TEACH THE WILL OF GOD WHICH WAS REVEALED TO ISRAEL.

When Moses gave the Law to our ancestors, with one voice they answered: "We will obey it and ever guard it." They have adhered to this noble promise for thousands of years. There were times when they became faithless, but soon, when misfortune opened their eyes, they gladly returned again to their religion, for only in faithful adherence to it could they find true happiness. So convinced were they of its sublime truths that they would rather suffer hatred, hardships, persecution and death than forsake it. God has created man to be happy, and to become morally perfect, and to this end he has revealed to us his divine law. If we wish to realize the blessings which God holds forth to us, then we must never forget the truths nor cease to practice the virtues nor fail to teach the lessons of our holy religion. There is no law like unto his, no law to take its place.

"Undoubtedly the revealed law is infinitely more authentic than that moral system which is framed by ethical writers, and denominated the natural law; because one is the law of Nature, expressly declared so to be by God himself, the other is only what by the assistance of human reason, we *imagine* to be that law. If we could be as *certain* of the latter as of the former, both would have an equal authority, but *until then they can never be put in competition together.*"—*Blackstone.*

1. Remember ye the law of Moses my servant, which I commanded unto him in Horeb for all Israel, with the statutes and judgments. (Malachi iii. 22.)

2. He showeth his word unto Jacob, his statutes and his judgments unto Israel. (Psalms cxlvii. 19.)

3. And God spake all these words, saying:

I. I am the Lord thy God, who brought thee out of the land of Egypt, out of the house of bondage.

II. Thou shalt have no other gods before me. Thou shalt not

make unto thee any graven image, or any likeness of anything that is in the heaven, above or that is in the earth beneath, or that is in the water under the earth. Thou shalt not bow down to them, nor serve them, for I the Lord thy God am a jealous God, visiting the iniquities of the fathers upon the children unto the third and fourth generations of them that hate me; and showing mercy unto the thousandth generation of them that love me and keep my commandments.

III. Thou shalt not take the name of the Lord thy God in vain, for the Lord will not hold him guiltless that taketh his name in vain.

IV. Remember the Sabbath-day to keep it holy. Six days shalt thou labor and do all thy work, but the seventh day is the Sabbath-day of the Lord thy God; on it thou shalt not do any work, thou nor thy son, nor thy daughter, nor thy man-servant, nor thy maid-servant, nor thy cattle, nor thy stranger that is within thy gates. For in six days the Lord made heaven and earth, the sea and all that is in them, and rested on the seventh day; therefore the Lord blessed the Sabbath-day and hallowed it.

V. Honor thy father and thy mother that thy days may be long upon the land which the Lord thy God giveth thee.

VI. Thou shalt not kill.

VII. Thou shalt not commit lewdness.

VIII. Thou shalt not steal.

IX. Thou shalt not bear false witness against thy neighbor.

X. Thou shalt not covet thy neighbor's house, thou shalt not covet thy neighbor's wife, nor his man-servant nor his maid-servant, nor his ox, nor his ass, nor anything that is thy neighbor's. (Exodus xx. 1-16.)

4. Behold, the Lord our God hath shown us his glory and his greatness, and we have heard his voice out of the midst of the fire, we have seen this day that God doth talk with man, and he liveth. Go thou near, and hear all that the Lord our God shall say, and speak thou unto us all that the Lord our God shall speak unto thee; and we will hear it and do it, and the Lord heard the voice of your

words, when ye spake unto me; and the Lord said unto me, I have heard the voice of the words of this people, which they have spoken unto thee, they have well said all they have spoken. O that there were such a heart in them, that they would fear me and keep my commandments always that it might be well with them, and with their children forever. (Deuteronomy v. 21, 24, 26.)

X.—IN ALWAYS FULFILLING THESE DUTIES LIES THE REALIZATION OF THE MISSION OF OUR RELIGION.

The mission of our religion is to make us realize all the benefits with which God has blessed us It bids us to strive with all the powers which he has endowed us to bring on that glorious time when all men will live together in unity and peace, when all men will unite in worshiping only the one holy God, and when the spirit of enlightenment will reign supreme. The realization of this lofty mission lies in our own hands. If we live up to the teachings of our religion, and by examples and words show others the necessity and the benefits of leading a pure and holy life, it will not be long before the common fatherhood of God and the common brotherhood of men will be acknowledged as the guiding principle of men in the actions of all intelligent beings.

"It is not Israel's political restoration, the re-establishment or the coming of a redeeming Messiah, which the Bible promises or predicts. It is a final and universal triumph of truth, righteousness, liberty and justice to which the prophets point. Every person contributing to the achievement of this great purpose is a Messiah and a messenger of the Most High. The habitable world must become one holy land, every city a Jerusalem, every house a temple, every table an altar, every person a priest of the Most High. This is the kingdom of God, the hope of mankind, our mission."—I. M. Wise.

1. Then will I sprinkle clean water upon you, and ye shall be

clean from all your impurities, and from all your idols will I cleanse you. A new heart also will I give you, and a new spirit will I put within you, and I will take away the heart of stone out of your flesh, and I will give you a heart of flesh. (Ezekiel xxxv. 25, 26.)

2. Behold, the days come, saith the Lord, that I will make a new covenant with the house of Israel, and with the house of Judah; not according to the covenant that I made with their fathers on the day that I took them by the hand to bring them out of the land of Egypt; which my covenant they broke, although I was a husband unto them, saith the Lord. But this shall be the covenant that I will make with the house of Israel, after those days, saith the Lord, I will put my law in their inward parts, and write it in their hearts; and will be their God, and they shall be my people. And they shall teach no more every man his neighbor, and every man his brother, saying, Know the Lord, for they shall all know me, from the least of them unto the greatest of them, saith the Lord, for I will forgive their iniquity, and I will remember their sin no more. Thus saith the Lord, who giveth the sun for a light by day, and the ordinances of the moon and of the stars for a light by night, which divideth the sea when the waves thereof roar, the Lord of hosts is his name. If these ordinances depart from before me, saith the Lord, then the seed of Israel also shall cease from being a nation before me forever. (Jeremiah xxxi. 31–36.)

3. As for me this is my covenant with them, saith the Lord; my spirit that is upon thee and my words which I have put in thy mouth shall not depart out of thy mouth, nor out of the mouth of thy children, nor out of the mouth of thy children's children, from henceforth unto all eternity, saith the Lord. (Isaiah lix. 21.)

4. In those days, and at that time, will I cause the branch of righteousness to grow up unto David; and he shall execute judgment and righteousness in the land. In those days shall Judah be saved, and Jerusalem shall dwell safely, and this is the name wherewith she shall be called, the Lord is our Righteousness. (Jeremiah xxxiii. 15, 16.)

5. But in the last days it shall come to pass that the mountain of the house of the Lord shall be established in the top of the mountains, and it shall be exalted above the hills, and people shall flow unto it. And many nations shall come, and say, Come and let us go up to the mountain of the Lord, and to the house of the God of Jacob, and he will teach us of his ways, and we will walk in his paths, for the Law shall go forth out of Zion, and the word of the Lord from Jerusalem. And he shall judge among many people, and rebuke strong nations afar off; and they shall beat their swords into plowshares and their spears into pruning-hooks; nations shall not lift up sword against nation, neither shall they learn war any more. But they shall sit every man under his vine and under his fig tree, and none shall make them afraid, for the mouth of the Lord of Hosts hath spoken it. (Michah iv. 1–4.)

6. Arise, shine, for the light is come, and the glory of the Lord is risen upon thee. For, behold, the darkness shall cover the earth, and gross darkness the people, but the Lord shall arise upon thee, and his glory shall be seen upon thee. And the Gentiles shall come to thy light and kings to the brightness of thy rising. (Isaiah lx. 1–3.)

7. For the earth shall be filled with the knowledge of the glory of the Lord, as the waters cover the sea. (Habakkuk ii. 14.)

8. For then will I turn to the people a pure language that they may all call upon the name of the Lord, to serve him with one consent. (Zephaniah iii. 9.)

9. All the ends of the world shall remember and turn unto the Lord, and all the kindreds of the nations shall worship before thee. For the kingdom is the Lord's and he is the governor among the nations. (Psalms xxii. 28, 29.)

10. And the Lord shall be king over all the earth, in that day shall there be one Lord, and his name one. (Zechariah xiv. 9.)

THE END.

www.ingramcontent.com/pod-product-compliance
Lightning Source LLC
Chambersburg PA
CBHW020155170426
43199CB00010B/1054